IGNITE *your* Purpose

ENLIGHTENING STORIES THAT WILL HELP YOU
FIND TRUE MEANING IN YOUR LIFE

INTRODUCTION BY

Lady JB Owen

Founder and CEO of Ignite Publishing™
and JBO Global Inc.™

Peter Giesin

Co-Founder and Chief Technology Officer of
Ignite Publishing™ and Longevity Coach

Mimi Safiyah

Lead Editor Ignite Publishing™

FOREWORD BY

Douglas Ivanovich

CEO & Executive Producer of WP1 Concerts™, Executive Producer for 1-Earth GPS™,
Executive Director for Storm Aid Fountation, Inc.

FEATURED AUTHORS

Kjirsten Sigmund

Speaker, Author, Teacher,
Thought Leader, and CEO

Peter Giesin

Cofounder and CTO at
Ignite Publishing™, Longevity
Coach, Author, and Adventurer.

ADDITIONAL FEATURED AUTHORS

BELINDA LEE SCHROEDER • ERIC LG LONGORIA • K.R. ROSSER
KANIKA ROSE RANEY • KATHY A. STUBBS • LADY JB OWEN
LIORA KARPS • LORENA LEE • LORETTA MITCHELL • NICOLE MIXDORF
NICOLE SHANTEL FREEMAN • RANDY DYCK • SHARNI QUINN • TINA HATCH
XILA C. HOPE • YELIZ RUZGAR

PUBLISHED BY IGNITE PUBLISHING™

IGN*TE™
your
Purpose

YOUR PURCHASE SUPPORTS CHARITY

Online profits made from Ignite books go to the *Ignite Humanity Classrooms of Hope*, a charity initiative Ignite has created with other charity partners. The money made from every online book sale goes toward building schools in rural and impoverished areas. Ignite is proud to be supporting and aiding literacy around the world. If you would like to donate, [click here](https://fundraise.classroomofhope.org/ignite-moments). Every book purchased makes a difference.

WRITE FOR IGNITE

We trust that after finishing this book, Ignite Moments™ will become a part of your vocabulary. You'll begin to think about your own Ignite Moments and the times in your life when you felt ignited to live a different way. If sharing your story feels important, or the idea of writing your Ignite Moment for others to enjoy is percolating to the surface, please reach out to us. We believe every person has a story, and every story deserves to be read. If your words are longing to come forth, we want to be there for you to make it happen. Our desire is to Ignite a billion lives through a billion words and share seven billion Ignite Moments around the globe.

GET TO KNOW IGNITE.

Over seven hundred authors have come to us and we have made them international best-sellers in both our compilation books and their own solo projects. People who were terrified to write have succeeded and created outstanding books. Authors who have struggled with writer's block have become victorious. Individuals who longed to be published but didn't know how to begin have reached best-seller status in a matter of months — delighted, triumphant, and empowered. From homemakers to teenagers, nomads to millionaires, we have systematically assisted authors in fulfilling their writing goals and reaching their sought-after dreams.

We want to be there to help you become published. Should you desire to write your Ignite Moment or have an idea for a full book of your own, let us be the ones to help reach your goal. As the leader of empowerment publishing we know how to take your book and bring it to the world to reach precisely the person who needs to read exactly what you have to share. Our programs are easy, fun, efficient, and we never own your content or collect royalties. Your story is yours. Our job is to help you share it with as many people as possible.

Learn more about how you can become a published author here: www.igniteyou.life

GET IGNITE'S
100 WRITING AFFIRMATIONS
EBOOK FOR FREE

Ignite your writing with these inspiring affirmations that were designed to unleash the superstar writer in you. Within this complimentary eBook, you'll find powerful affirmations for you to use daily to gain confidence in yourself and your writing. If you want to get access to this amazing resource, use the QR code below to gain access.

Other international best-selling compilation books
by IGNITE for you to enjoy:

———————

Ignite Your Life for Women

Ignite Your Female Leadership

Ignite Your Parenting

Ignite Your Life for Men

Ignite Your Life for Conscious Leaders

Ignite Your Health and Wellness

Ignite Your Adventurous Spirit

Ignite Female Change Makers

Ignite the Modern Goddess

Ignite Happiness

Ignite Love

Ignite Your Inner Spirit

Ignite the Entrepreneur

Ignite Possibilities

Ignite the Hunger in You

Ignite Your Life for Women (2nd Edition)

Ignite Possibilities (2nd edition)

Ignite Your Wisdom

Ignite Forgiveness

Ignite Your Faith

Ignite Your Courage

PURPOSE AUTHORS

Belinda Schroeder

Eric Longoria

JB Owen

Kanika Rose Raney

Karen R. Rosser

Kathy Stubbs

Kjirsten Sigmund

Liora Karps

Lorena Norman

Loretta M. Mitchell

Nicole Mixdorf

Nicole S. Freeman

Peter Giesin

Randy Dyck

Sharni Quinn

Tina Hatch

Xila C. Hope

Yeliz Rugar

Published and printed by Ignite Publishing™
5569-47th Street Red Deer, AB
Canada, T4N1S1 1-877-677-6115

Editor-in-Chief JB Owen
Book and Cover design by Dania Zafar, Katie Smetherman, and Sinisa Poznanovic
Edited by Alex Blake, Michiko Couchman, Mimi Safiyah, Sarah Cross, and Zoe Wong.

Designed in Canada, Printed in China

ISBN: 978-1-7923-8769-2

Ordering Information: Quantity sales. Special discounts are available on quantity purchases by corporations, associations, and others. For details, contact the publisher at the above address. Programs, products, or services provided by the authors are found by contacting them directly.

Dedication

*Ignite Your Purpose is dedicated to every person on the planet,
for we all exist with a purpose.*

PETER GIESIN

*To my beloved wife, In the vast tapestry of life, where destinies interweave
and paths crisscross, I found you—a beacon of hope, love, and endless
inspiration. Your essence brings color to my world, turning everyday moments
into timeless memories. With every beat of my heart, I am reminded of the
serendipity that brought us together and the unwavering bond that continues
to grow. This dedication, though a mere collection of words, is but a feeble
attempt to encapsulate the profound gratitude and love I hold for you. May
every page we turn together be filled with joy, adventure, and the kind of love
that stories are built upon. Here's to our forever.*

BELINDA SCHROEDER

*For Nina and George, my darling parents, who have given me a lifetime of
inspiration to be the best person I can be. And for giving life to my sweet
brother, who continues to be a force for love in our family.*

ERIC LONGORIA

*Thank you to everyone who has been there with me and had my back (you
know who you are). Each connection I have made is a part of who I am and my
story. Thank you, God, for not letting me give up.*

KANIKA ROSE RANEY

*I would like to dedicate this chapter to my beautiful, bold, intelligent, and
selfless mother, Vivian Raney. My biggest cheerleader, supporting my every
dream, big and small, and serving as a compass as I navigate the journey of
life. She is the epitome of love, generosity, and sacrifice, fulfilling her purpose
as a mother through unconditional love, never-ending patience, bountiful
compassion, and infinite wisdom. Because of her, I am. Because of her, I can
choose to live a purpose-driven life.*

Karen R. Rosser

I dedicate my story to the myriad of people worldwide who are embracing intentional living. Those who are in pursuit of self-discovery, self-connection, and living a purposeful life.

Kathy Stubbs

I dedicate my chapter in Ignite Your Purpose to those who have supported me on my journey. My thanks to family, friends, teachers, mentors, and the unseen spirits that have helped me realize possibilities and my own potential.

Kjirsten Sigmund

I would like to dedicate this chapter to all sentient beings.

Liora Karps

Dedicated to my husband, Shaun. A quiet and humble man who displayed great strength, inner sense, and integrity above all else. My soulmate and anchor. To my children Idan and Ashira, you continue to guide and inspire me daily! To my sister Dana, I am grateful for you every single day! To my family, I continue to draw strength from your constant love and support, to my friends who make me laugh even in the darkest times, and to my community who wrapped us in a beautiful blanket of comfort when our world was falling apart. To Maria, thank you for your ever-present support and ensuring our home runs smoothly! To Claudia, without your care, guidance, and friendship, I don't know how I would have made it through, and to Trevor, thank you for constantly pushing me out of my comfort zone to truly live with feeling and purpose as I navigate this new reality.

Lorena Norman

I dedicate this to those who seek illumination. I am abundantly grateful and humbled by my family and friends, who have continued to support my ever-changing journey. To all of my ancestors who have departed this realm and continue to guide me, thank you. I love you all.

Loretta M. Mitchell

I dedicate this chapter to my husband, Jim, my sons Jesse and Christopher, my grandchildren Korie and Calix, and my heavenly daughter, Heather. You have all inspired me to do my best!

Nicole S. Freeman

With dedication to my two most cherished blessings and sources of joy, my daughters, Alli and Ainsli.

Nicole Mixdorf

This story is dedicated to the loving memory of my sweet daddy, Papa, Alita, Zadie, cousin Sylvia, and my babies, who are all with me in spirit.

Randy Dyck

"To my twin, Gerry: 'Racers ready!' These words rang out in everything we did, became, and are. Through this challenging time, you didn't just race beside me—you lifted me, allowing me to match your pace. You let me win when you could have soared ahead, and through sports, runs, and rides, you rekindled my spirit. More than a brother, you were my anchor, my guiding star in navigating adversity. Your unwavering faith reignited my drive, pushing me toward greatness and helping me rediscover my purpose.
This book is for you, my hero."

Sharni Quinn

To my parents, who have always supported me, loved me, believed in me, and encouraged me to "do what makes me happy" and live my purpose.

Tina Hatch

To my parents, who have given so much to me, and to my wife, who is a light in the world. To my kids, who bring me so much joy. To Dr. Lynne Goodhart, my mentor and French professor who helped me find my voice, and to my therapist who lovingly held space for me when I came out. To the readers who see a part of themselves in my story, may you find courage and love in these pages.

Xila C. Hope

The story Pierce the Silence is dedicated to the voices of grandmothers who speak life and purpose to every situation. Lubertha Donley is known to many as granny, who is quick to use a gentle tongue to break a bone. Yet, her figurative language is also how many pursue their purpose in life. So, Granny, although you didn't want anything written about you in this book, you have a whole chapter referencing how your voice can influence generations!

TESTIMONIALS FROM AUTHORS

The Ignite team does a fantastic job of taking solo stories and putting them together. It was great to collaborate in the group discussions and masterminds because I had the opportunity to gain perspective that made a difference in my writing. The team enjoys what they do, and they really pour their hearts into making sure you have the best story.

—Eric Longoria

Collaborating with the Ignite Publishing team and fellow authors on this book has been an incredible journey. The expertise and guidance of JB and the editors truly brought out the essence of my Ignite moment, weaving it into a captivating narrative that engages and lingers. The thoughtful and meticulous Ignite writing process, leaving no detail unattended, was matched only by the warmth of the supportive community of writers, editors, and the entire Ignite team. This experience not only birthed a remarkable book but also enriched my growth as a storyteller.

—Kanika Rose Raney

Writing in *Ignite Your Purpose* allowed me to embrace a profound sense of fulfillment within me. The power of living life purposefully has truly been an incredible journey of growth and self-discovery. Each day of my life presents opportunities for me to foster a renewed sense of contentment and direction.

—Karen R. Rosser

Thank you to Lady JB and the Ignite Team for all your guidance and support in helping me to put my feelings and story into the perfect words!

—Liora Karps

I had never heard of Ignite Publishing until I asked a friend how to go about getting a book published. She introduced me to Lady JB, and here I am. Many thanks to the Ignite team for all the guidance and support for this writing adventure. I have had an exciting journey fulfilling my dream of writing in an inspirational book for humanity.

—Loretta M. Mitchell

I am most grateful for the Ignite family and the seamless writing process. The passion and love is shown throughout the whole process.

—Nicole S. Freeman

This is my second time writing with Ignite, and I am just as pleased and impressed as I was before! The Ignite team is fantastic and made the process of flushing out my idea, editing, publishing, and marketing the book easy and fun. Thank you for such a wonderful experience!

—Nicole Mixdorf

My literary journey reached an extraordinary turning point when I had the chance to connect with JB and Peter on a transformational hike in Vancouver. From the moment we met, it was clear that Ignite Publishing was not just about publishing books; it was about forging connections, understanding an author's vision, and turning dreams into reality. JB's leadership and insightful expertise created a synergy that ignited my project with new energy and focus. The entire staff at Ignite Publishing carried this same ethos, working diligently to provide support at every stage. Their collaborative spirit and unerring dedication to excellence transformed my manuscript into a published work I'm proud to call my own. I cannot express enough gratitude to JB, Peter, and the team at Ignite Publishing for lighting the path of my literary success!

—Randy Dyck

Working with Lady JB Owen and the Ignite Team has been an inspiration. The writing support, caring, nurturing, and high vibes I received while co-authoring the Ignite Your Purpose book have been truly heartwarming. I feel so grateful and have loved this whole experience!

—Sharni Quinn

Publishing with Ignite has been a wonderful experience. The editors are encouraging and helpful. I enjoyed the experience of getting to know other authors in the compilation book and having a supportive space each week with them.

—Tina Hatch

I became an international best-selling author with the Ignite Your Faith anthology. Therefore, I knew I could trust the process with this publisher again to bring life to my words. The subject matter I write about is very important and dear to my heart. So, it was imperative that I shared it with a team that had a common purpose of impacting communities around the world. Thank you, Ignite, for creating writing opportunities for individuals like me.

—Xila C. Hope

Contents

WHAT IS AN IGNITE BOOK?

Ignite Publishing has been the leader of Empowerment Publishing for the past half-decade. We sprung onto the scene with a desire to disrupt the publishing industry with books that only tell powerful, authentic, heart-felt stories designed to change lives. As we surpassed our twentieth compilation book, with over 700+ authors published, we feel we are doing just that: empowering others, igniting lives, and making a massive difference on the planet that will inspire generations for centuries to come.

The very word Ignite signifies the intention of our books and describes the goal behind each story we share. We see our books as gifts to the world, igniting ideas, thoughts, feelings, and desires in those who read them. Every book we publish is created with the intention to elevate, transform, and Ignite the reader toward something greater within themselves. We believe that our books and the stories inside them connect hearts, foster love, bridge gaps, and form a deeper understanding within us. The wonderful stories inside our books are divinely shared so that they become a beacon of empowerment for every person on the planet.

Ignite believes that stories and the genuine sharing of them is the key not only to bringing people together but to healing humanity on a global scale. Stories speak directly to the heart of the reader and touch them in a heartfelt and profound way. Honest and authentic stories open the mind and expand compassion, foster connection, and bring forth the kind of joy that we all desire to have. Stories showcase our commonalities and show how we are more alike than different. They speak of the common denominator we all know, the beautiful human experience.

Each story in this book has been created to encourage you on a deeper level. They are designed to awaken your mind while speaking directly to your heart and instilling a new sense of courage and purpose. As you begin reading an Ignite story, you will find that each one begins with an inspiring Power Quote. It is an empowering statement designed to push you forward and challenge you to break outside your comfort zone. Power quotes are phrases that offer insight and motivation. They are meaningful statements intended to Ignite ideas, spark actions, and evoke change. Every Power Quote is written to activate something in you, so you can be all that you desire to become and, ideally, Ignite another person.

Since this book is all about igniting one's life, each Power Quote is designed to activate a deeper connection within you. They are written with the intention that whatever you have gone through, or are going through, you can use your inner knowing, to move forward to overcome what might be in your way. The wonderful thing about each story is that it is unique, personal, and intimate. A person's path is unique to them, but the power behind their experience is universal among us all. These stories show a connection to something greater: ourselves. They shine a light on the power within us with the hope they will inspire you.

After the Power Quote, you will find the author's Personal Intention. These are the individual insights and genuine wishes the author wants to share with you, as well as their intention for what you will gain from reading their authentic story. Each author came into this book with a desire to Ignite something in you, and they share that lovingly in their Personal Intention. From the very beginning, they want you to know they want their story to indeed Ignite something greater in you.

After the Personal Intention, you will read the author's transformational Ignite Moment. It is a genuine sharing of the author's journey and how they emerge through it with a greater understanding of themselves. Through their unique experiences and circumstances, the authors explain how their Ignite Moment transformed them, awakened them, and set them on a new trajectory in life. They reveal their honest feelings and share their personal discoveries. They give an insightful account of the exact pivotal moment when an inner awakening created a valuable understanding that there was more within themselves.

We all have Ignite Moments that change us, define us, and set us forth on a wonderful new journey of inner exploration. The stories in this book are derived from those moments and are told in the most endearing and empowering way. They show us that life-altering situations are designed to impact us in a way that inspires us to step into the person we were born to become. Ignite Moments are universal and transcend all barriers. They allow us to be more connected on a deeper level, showing how we are all One in many ways.

To take each story to another level, you will discover the authors' share exciting Ignite Action Steps at the end of every chapter. They want to provide doable actions that you can use to benefit yourself. Each Action Step is an idea, process, or practice they have used to succeed in their own life. The goal is for you to implement an action step into your life and provoke positive change. Each Ignite Action Step is different and unique, just like you, and each has proven to have amazing results when done diligently and consistently.

As you sit down to read this book, know that it is not required that you read it in the traditional way by starting at the beginning and reading through to the end. Many readers flip to a page at random and read from there, trusting that the page they landed on holds the exact story they need to read. Others glance over the table of contents, searching for the title that resonates with them. Some readers will go directly to a story recommended by a friend. However you decide to read this book, we trust it will be right for you. We know that you may read it from cover to cover in one single sitting or pick it up and put it down a dozen times. The way you read an Ignite book is as personal as every story in it, so we give you complete permission to enjoy it in whatever way fits you.

We ask that if a story touches you in some way or inspires your heart, you reach out and tell the author. Your words will mean the world to them. Since our book is all about igniting humanity, we want to foster more of that among all of us. Feel free to share your sentiments with the authors by using their contact information at the end of the book. There isn't an Ignite author who wouldn't love to hear from you and know that somehow their story positively impacted your life. And, if a story speaks to you profoundly, we encourage you to share it with someone special who may need to read it, as that story may just be the exact thing they need to help Ignite their life.

We know you will find a part of your story reflected in the wisdom, wishes, and dreams of the many authors here. Somewhere within these pages will be a reflection of your journey and the Ignite Moments you have felt. We know this because Ignite stories represent the stories in all of us. It doesn't matter where you live, your skin color, gender, or how much money you have in your pocket; Ignite stories reflect everyone. They are stories of the human condition; they touch the very essence of what makes us human and our powerful human experience. They bring us together, showing us that our stories do not define us but, instead, refine who we can become.

As you turn the page, we want to welcome you to the Ignite family. We are excited for what is about to happen because we know the stories in this book will inspire transformation. As you dive into the upcoming pages, a million different emotions will fill your heart, and a kindred spirit with our authors will be established. We know that this will be a book that both awakens and inspires, transforms, and motivates.

May you be loved and supported from this page forward, and may all your Ignite Moments be filled with both joyful lessons and heart-filled blessings.

Lady JB Owen

Founder and CEO of Ignite

WELCOME TO
IGNITE YOUR PURPOSE

In the silence spaces between the incessant hum of our daily lives, a quiet question whispers, *What is my purpose?* This is not a question of existentialism, but one of clarity. Throughout the ages of history, from the great thinkers to the everyday person, the search for purpose has been an intrinsic pursuit. Although, what if the journey to discover *why you are here* is not so much a search outward, but a flame waiting to be ignited from within?

Welcome, dear reader, to *Ignite Your Purpose!*

This book is not just a reading of words; it's an odyssey. A pilgrimage through the historical labyrinths of purpose, unveiling its myriad interpretations, dissecting its very essence, and lighting up its many facets that have been revered across cultures, religions, and epochs.

Purpose is not merely a job description or a fleeting passion. It's the deep-seated reason for our very existence, an ethereal call from the Universe that resonates with the core of our being. When we align with it, we don't just live; we thrive. We become luminous beacons, casting ripples of positivity, innovation, and inspiration everywhere we go.

Within these pages, you will embark on a self-reflective journey nudged by personal prompts and introspective exercises designed to delve into your psyche as well as awaken the dormant flames of a great purpose residing in you. These are not random exercises. They are the work you need to do to awaken introspection and those insightful experiences that have been given to you.

Throughout the journey, you'll also bear witness to intimate anecdotes from numerous authors who faced crossroads and epiphanies in their lives. These are not just stories; they are Ignite Moments—profound, transformative instances where the beautiful concept of purpose bursts forth as a palpable, driving force.

Each story they share is a testament that purpose isn't just a luxury for the chosen few, it's an attainable reality for all. However, the path is not always adorned with signposts and directions. The discovery of your purpose demands courage, vulnerability, and an unwavering belief in oneself. It is a quest that once you feel ready to take on, nothing can stop you until you find Purpose itself.

We look forward to supporting you in your endeavor to learn more and connect with the purpose residing inside of you. May turning the next page unlock an array of answers, information, and clarity around your purpose. Allow each story you read and each action step you take, bring bring you closer to discovering the Divine purpose that has been gifted and given to you. Your purpose is your light and the spark that ignites the flame for someone else.

Finding your purpose will change the world!

"The things that excite you are not random. They are connected to your Purpose. Follow them."

—*Thinkgrowprosper*

A WORLD ABOUNDING
WITH PURPOSE

Close your eyes and imagine for a moment...

Step into a Universe teeming with potential, where every horizon beckons with new opportunities and every heartbeat echos with undying passion. This is a world painted with the bright hues of hope and aspiration, where every individual is part of a tapestry filled with dreams and ambitions. Each morning, the sun rises, casting away shadows and radiating boundless possibilities, every breath invigorating, and every step filled with anticipation.

The world is alive and pulsating, humming with the harmonious symphony of human collaboration. Streets are bustling with innovative ideas, joyous laughter, and the unmistakable sounds of progress. Buildings rise, not just as mere structures, but as symbols of human ingenuity and determination. The air is thick with excitement, the constant pursuit of greatness, and a deep-rooted desire to create, evolve, and inspire.

In this luminous realm, children are born with excitement in their eyes, brimming with curiosity. Their questions are filled with wonder, probing into the mysteries of the Universe, the magic of togetherness, and the dazzling dance of connectedness amongst us all. They eagerly ask, "What can we achieve?" Realizing life here as a grand adventure, a celebration of emotions, fervor, and creativity.

You can feel the boundless rush of such a purposeful existence. The elation of a world where dreams not only exist but set the very sky ablaze? Here love knows no bounds, fearlessly venturing into the uncharted territories of the heart. It's a world where every story instills hope, every endeavor offers collaboration, and each person is a beautiful stroke on the canvas of humanity.

Now, open your eyes and take heart, for that is the realm where purpose knows no bounds! That is where dreams and desires are fulfilled and where those living on purpose activate a greater experience of life itself. The joy of living on purpose weaves its way through every corner of creation and we feel the rise of humankind.

Purpose has made such a place possible.

Purpose, with its rich and profound implications, is more than just a word or concept; it is a deep-rooted force, acting as a stabilizing anchor in the unpredictable and often stormy seas of life. This elusive, yet palpable essence, isn't merely a compass pointing the way or a distant star illuminating the night; it pulses with the very heart of human existence, painting our shared journey with vibrant shades of emotion, driving passions, and unyielding perseverance. It's the symphony to which humanity's story has been set, a rhythm that resonates across eras, influencing every thought, action, and monumental shift in our collective destiny.

Looking back at our forbears, the luminance of purpose was evident even when surrounded by the harsh uncertainties of a world still in the throes of formation. Amidst dense forests echoing with unseen dangers, beyond the instinctive needs of hunger or the adrenaline-spiked fears of predators, there thrived a deeper, more profound sentiment—the burgeoning spirit of purpose. This spirit led our early ancestors to one of the most pivotal moments in human history: the taming of fire. More than a mere means to fend off the numbing cold or ward away nocturnal threats, this discovery forged a communal nucleus. Drawn to its radiant warmth, these ancient humans huddled, not just seeking physical comfort but, more significantly, a space to weave tales of valiant quests, aspirations, and dreams. Those stories, whispered from one generation to the next, sewed the primary fabric of our human identity, heralding the inception of shared values and cultural identities.

The voyage of purpose was far from static. It was dynamic, urging humanity to perpetually seek, innovate, and transcend boundaries. No longer content with just subsisting, our ancestors transcended the ordinary. They meticulously crafted tools, turning rudimentary stones and bones into masterful extensions of their intent. They gazed upon the untamed wilderness not as mere spectators, but as visionaries, seeing potential where none appeared. This led them to plant the initial seeds of agriculture, transforming nomadic wanderers into settled communities. Those nascent settlements, bathed in the collective purpose of their inhabitants, became the foundations of the world's first great civilizations.

Within those sprawling narratives of civilizations were individuals whose very existence became synonymous with purpose: Gallilio, Scortoes, Da Vinci, Newton, Jefferson, Eddison, Linchion, Parks, Hill, Pastuer, King, Kennedy, Angelou, Thatcher, Whinfrey, and the list goes on. These and many others have made their purpose a driving force that has shaped humanity from history until today. They have shown what magnificent and powerful outcomes can be made from knowing *why you are here.*

Living on purpose acts as a personal compass, urging us to aspire, achieve, and constantly push the boundaries of what's possible. Countless individuals, from every corner of the globe, during different eras, from diverse backgrounds, immersed in every culture, have embodied this purpose-driven spirit. They have shown us that when we act with purpose, seeking to better ourselves and others, there's no dream too distant or goal too unattainable. They have revealed that anyone and everyone has the ability to impact and ignite the world when purpose is their driving force.

Now it is your turn to make your name synonymous with purpose and add your unique imprint to the many others who have shaped and molded our world. As you live your purpose you influence history and lay the foundations for endless possibilities to unfold. You join the many others who have found their meaning and made the commitment to a future brimming with unlimited existence.

WHY PURPOSE MATTERS

It is only recently that finding one's purpose has become trendy and on point. Although the facets of purpose are often discussed in books, movies, and media, the essence of purpose is frequently misunderstood. We often attach our purpose to our belongings, or our achievements in life, such as having kids, buying a house, or fulfilling the status quo that has been imparted to us from a young age. Yet, our purpose is so much deeper than all of these things. Your purpose helps you impact the world and leave your legacy. It is what *feeds your soul* and invigorates your spirit. Your purpose is the part of you that brings meaning to everything you do.

Knowing your purpose gives you a deeper understanding of yourself, It is like a magnet from within, pushing you forward toward your true destiny. Acting with such desire enlightens those around you—it is infectious and contagious. When people see you living in your purpose, it fuels them to embark on their own voyage of self-enlightenment. They become inspired by your passion, by your zest for life—they want to see the world through a more meaningful lens. This creates a ripple effect of ingenuity and a surge of benefits for others to learn from. When we impact those around us, we enliven the next generations with endless opportunities. We create a domino effect that creates a beautiful manifestation of transformation that positively influences everything that it touches. By knowing your purpose and living it out each day, you have the ability to impact humanity on a grander scale. Your purpose helps to change fundamental aspects of humankind that are yearning for growth, and aspiring to evolve into something much greater than what they originally knew.

When we embrace our purpose, and allow it to seep into every inch of our being, we ignite a spark within us that illuminates and enriches the lives of others. Once we step into our untapped power we are poised for anything. We exude a power that is so transcendent that it captivates everyone who stumbles onto our path. People are attracted to those living on purpose—their direction leads those lost to find their own direction. Purpose-driven action fosters more of the same. Soon, many are following your lead and purposefulness is spreading like wildfire.

Your purpose is a gift that you first give to yourself and then share with the world. It is a Divine calling that has been with you since you were born, and yet it has been waiting patiently for the right moment to unveil itself to you, a moment when you are open, willing, and ready to receive it. Your purpose carries with it a wisdom that only you will be able to master. It has been uniquely crafted to fit every inch of your being, knowing you intrinsically. Every aspect of your purpose has the power for you to create something meaningful. This is what makes your purpose so profound, so monumental. In living your purpose you give the gift of being on purpose to everyone you meet.

Take a moment right now to ask yourself if you know your purpose. Analyze your actions and decide if they have been guided and purpose-driven, or if they have been in search of and questioning the meaning of your life. Whichever answer you declare is the right answer for where you are right now—knowing it or discovering it. Both are correct. Both are beautiful. Living on purpose or finding your purpose all leads to a life of meaning and direction, of clarity and conviction, of peace, love, and joy. All the things we blessedly find meaningful.

When you walk in purpose, you collide with Destiny.

—*Ralph Buchanan*

Take the journey right now in intimately becoming more invested in your purpose and knowing what was divinely designed for you. Ask yourself, *what do I think my purpose is,* and listen to the answer you hear. It may be a whisper, a faint sharing, or a tickle in your ear. It may be a raging call. A resounding reverberation in your soul. Whatever you hear, write it down and let it be the starting point of something grand and magnificent. Something personal and poignant. Let it be what moves you forward to the next great step you are about to take.

What do I think my purpose is?

_____

_____

_____

_____

_____

_____

_____

_____

_____

_____

_____

_____

If the words poured off the page or struggled to come out of the pen, not to worry. Whatever you wrote is perfect… now let's discover some more.

BECOMING YOUR PURPOSE

You may be intuitively wondering why a book about igniting your purpose has come into your hands—and why now.

The answer is simple… You are ready.

The world needs dreamers, doers, thinkers, and believers. People who are willing to tune into their inner symphonies and play their unique notes out loud. People like you. People who want more from thier life than the status quo and choose to make a difference unabashed. Up until now your purpose may have been elusive or unclear, yet you want to look deeper and are hungry for answers and more clarity.

Discovering one's purpose is a process and a quest. It isn't supposed to be easy; if it was, it wouldn't be considered as sacred as it is. It must be layered in the unfolding of who you are and wrapped in the makings of your willingness to find it despite the odds.

Michelangelo painted the Sistine Chapel despite numerous setbacks. It took 4 years for him to complete the 500-square-meter fresco of over three hundred figures while painting on the ceiling. The only way that was possible was because of his conviction to fulfill that purpose.

Nelson Mandela spent twenty-seven years in prison, only to be released and become the first democratically elected president of South Africa because of his reconciliation and advocacy for peace. His purpose was clear to him despite his circumstances.

Author and speaker, Joe Vitale has written over seventy books on various topics, such as marketing, business, spirituality, personal development, and visualization. His passion for the topic of purpose and sharing its value has yielded such impressive results even though there was a time in Joe's life when he was lost and homeless.

Michael Phelps, the famous American swimmer, has won twenty-eight Olympic medals, including twenty-three gold by living on his purpose for swimming, his faith in God, and his desire to help others. He was later scandalized in the news and criticized for his personal life yet he never let that stop him from surging forward and reaching his goals.

These are just a few examples that show the path to purpose is not always rosy or straight. One purpose may unfold like a labyrinth, the endpoint not clear or dotted with direction signs. Another, weaves and meanders through the lessons of life, admits the blessings, and clears challenges.

In truth, purpose shows up in all kinds of ways and is unique and specific to each and every person it touches. That is why no one book can tell you what your purpose is; it is for you to define. Your purpose is for you to know and reveal to yourself when you are ready and eager. It is already in you and a part of you. The journey is to awaken to it and bring it forth in your life.

Of course that sounds easier said than done and still can feel confusing and ambiguous. That is why it is helpful to begin looking for the clues that are evident in your life. From the moment you were born, your purpose has been encoded in you. Just like a tiny acorn seed has everything it needs to grow into a giant oak tree, you too inherently have all the abilities you need to execute your purpose.

You may need to do more, learn more, and give more, but the essence of your purpose is becoming more of who you already are.

That means now is the time to answer a few questions that will reveal the very information you require to know your purpose fully and wholeheartedly.

Find your WHY, and you'll find your WAY.

—John C. Maxwell

MAPPING OUT YOUR PURPOSE

If you are journeying through life searching for your purpose, we want to assure you that *you are not alone*. We have created many prompts to help you look deep within yourself to find the spark that awaits you, tap into its potential, and transform your life. These questions are those that will stir the caldron of what is possible and add kindling to the fire inside your aspirations. Answer them honestly while listening to the heart, not following the logic or the practicality in your head. Purpose is not what someone else is doing, or something you see on television. You can't find it out there, it is only within.

Think back to when you were young, a child, and felt unencumbered with responsibilities. What kinds of things did you love to do?

_____

_____

_____

_____

_____

_____

When you dreamed of your future, what feelings did you have?

_____

_____

_____

_____

_____

What made you the happiest when you were young?

_____

_____

_____

_____

_____

Now, think of your life today and ask yourself, what can I do for hours on end and just enjoy?

_____

_____

_____

_____

_____

What am I doing when I feel most alive and carefree?

_____

_____

_____

_____

_____

What am I passionate about?

_____

_____

_____

_____

_____

What am I talented at?

_____

_____

_____

_____

_____

_____

What do other people tell me I am good at?

_____

_____

_____

_____

_____

What do I think I am good at?

_____

_____

_____

_____

_____

What things do I do that make me smile?

_____

_____

_____

_____

_____

What do I most love about myself?

_____

_____

_____

_____

_____

What am I proud of?

_____

_____

_____

_____

_____

All of these questions are important so take your time and answer them fully. Don't rush through this process. Allow yourself to venture into the many layers that bring these answers to the surface with genuine clarity. See yourself in the best light, and focus on the positive parts that make you, you.

My unique qualities are...

_____

_____

_____

_____

_____

My core values are...

_____

_____

_____

_____

_____

If l was capable of doing my heart's desire I would be doing...

_____

_____

_____

_____

_____

Each realization you have about yourself is a vital aspect of your purpose, unfolding within you. Take a moment to recognize the preciousness of your answers and the gift each one brings. As you define your purpose, you will notice that there is a calling to expand beyond who you are at this present moment and seek even further.

What world issues concern me?

_____

_____

_____

_____

How can I help humanity?

_____

_____

_____

_____

_____

What challenges have I overcome that could inspire others?

_____

_____

_____

_____

_____

What wisdom have I gleaned that is valuable?

_____

_____

_____

_____

_____

Know that your purpose is interconnected to more then just you. A grand plan, of divine propositions, is always unfolding and you are a part of it. See the magic that is all around you in shining the light upon your path.

Things I find meaningful...

_____

_____

_____

_____

People who inspire me...

_____

_____

_____

_____

Where I want to spend my time...

_____

_____

_____

_____

_____

How I want to direct my energy...

_____

_____

_____

_____

_____

You decide your life. You always have a choice. If everything was perfectly aligned and all things were working for you what would your life look like?

_____

_____

_____

_____

_____

If everything was in alignment and you were guaranteed success, what would you be doing?

_____

_____

_____

_____

_____

If you could not fail, what would you achieve?

_____

_____

_____

_____

_____

Take a moment to look back and reflect on your answers and the clarity you have made. See the many commonalities you have shared and the silver thread throughout your answers. Notice where the theme of your purpose is right there on the page. Look over what you loved to do as a child and what you love to do now. Recognize how your emotions, desires, and wishes for yourself, mirror what you desire for others. Identify what you have always valued and what is an intrinsic aspect of your life. These are all the foundations of your purpose and what is inherently a part of you.

What do I notice about my answers?

_____

_____

_____

_____

_____

_____

_____

What seems clear and important to me?

_____

_____

_____

_____

_____

What feels like my purpose?

_____

_____

_____

_____

_____

If I were to write a succinct purpose statement it would be...

_____

_____

_____

_____

_____

_____

Living your purpose is pure satisfaction and bliss. Once you're able to see it with clarity and how deeply it is rooted in you, each day becomes a beautiful opportunity to be exactly that. There is no confusion because the directive is clear. You move in that direction, you settle for nothing less. You declare it to the world and the world delivers it in return.

Once you start living your purpose, encourage others to do the same. Be the one who ignites another to find their purpose. Lead by example and foster harmony. Focus on a world where each one of us is living in the epicenter of our purpose. Imagine the world that will be!

SEEING YOUR PURPOSE UNFOLD

As you navigate the labyrinth of life, embodying your true purpose becomes akin to unfurling a precious moment, an Ignite Moment, revealing insights and wisdom beautifully gathered on your personal journey. With the map of your grand scheme laid out, the time is ripe to set forth with a heart brimming with expectation and a spirit reverberating with resolute determination.

Embark on this discovery with the spirit of curiosity and remember that every step you take is a testament to the powerful force of intention. This is more than a mission; it is a vibrant masterpiece coming to life, a rich tapestry woven with golden threads of aspirations and bold strokes of effort.

You are not merely walking a path, you are carving it, creating a majestic panorama vibrant with hues of hope and shades of perseverance, where every endeavor is a burst of colors depicting the ceaseless dance of creation and realization. This journey is your canvas, where the vivid imagination of your heart meets the stark reality, transforming into a landscape bursting with possibility and pulsating with life.

The journey toward living out your purpose is laden with deeply personal and transformative experiences. As you will witness in the stories throughout this book, each one of us holds within our essence a reservoir of dreams and fervent desire to reach pinnacles of personal achievements.

Sharing the essence of your journey with the world becomes an act of beautiful vulnerability and powerful strength. It is an open invitation to others to delve deep within themselves, to connect with their hidden reserves of potential, and to dare to dream grand dreams. It is a testament to the world that when one rises, fueled by a burning purpose, a path unfolds before them, lit by the radiant glow of possibility and paved with golden opportunities.

In sharing, you build bridges of understanding, forging bonds with others on the journey of life, fostering a community where inspiration is the currency and where dreams are the north star guiding each individual on their path of purpose. Your journey, infused with the spirit of purpose, becomes a radiant light that ushers others, encouraging them to unearth the treasures buried within, embrace their true potential, and set forth on their own journey of discovery and actuality.

As you consume the stories in *Ignite Your Purpose*, you will witness a magnificent orchestra of purposes harmoniously unfolding. It is a grand mosaic where each individual, driven by their unique purpose, adds to the collective, creating a world we all want to live in.

In this sacred space where purposes converge and energies harmonize, we discover the true essence of life. Sharing becomes a celebration, a jubilant dance of joy, where each story, your story, resonates with others, fostering a rich culture of encouragement, understanding, and mutual growth.

As you step forth into the unfurling of your purposes, may you do so with a spirit aflame with passion, a heart open to the beauty, and a soul ready to embrace the fulfilling adventure of your purpose unfolding in all its magnificent splendor. It is a dance of dreams coming to fruition, a harmonious symphony of intertwined destinies, singing a glorious anthem of hope, inspiration, and boundless potential.

"Embrace your purpose, it's the harmony of dreams meeting potential."

—Peter Giesin

Doug Ivanovich

FOREWORD

DOUG IVANOVICH

*"From the tiniest grain of sand to the biggest of all galaxies,
everything has a purpose.*

*Your highest mission and purpose awaits you;
find it and embark on life's greatest adventure!"*

It is with a deep sense of gratitude and honor that I find myself composing this foreword for *Ignite Your Purpose*, the latest addition to the series of books under the inspiring theme of Ignite. To Ignite founder, author, and organizer JB Owen, I extend my heartfelt thanks for inviting me to contribute these words. As I undertake this task, I am reminded of the power of purpose, the very essence that propels us forward, lighting our path during both the best of times, as well as the most challenging of times.

In a world that often moves at a dizzying pace, where distractions abound, and the noise of daily life often drowns out the whispers of our inner selves, a book centered around the concept of purpose is not only relevant… It is essential. The *Ignite* series uniquely stirs the embers of our consciousness, urging us to cast aside the mundane and embrace the extraordinary. *Ignite Your Purpose* stands as a guiding beacon, illuminating the profound journey of self-discovery while helping us to nurture and actualize our lives.

Why focus on "purpose" in this series of Ignite books? It's a question that echoes with profound significance. Purpose is the fuel that ignites our aspirations and draws us toward our truest selves. Within these pages, readers will find a compass that will help guide them through the labyrinth of life, urging us all to question, reflect, and ultimately craft a life filled with inspiration, authenticity, and fulfillment.

As a writer and lecturer on the world's wisdom traditions, the subject of Purpose has always been both captivating and compelling. Throughout adulthood, a sense of unease persisted regarding those who asserted materialism's dominance over the spiritual. My inner and outer searches have led me, like many others, to an invisible source or power that extends far beyond the senses. This hunger for truth and longing to find a greater purpose has prompted a lifetime's investment in the exploration of life's deepest mysteries and meaning. My Ignite Moments always arose when crossing paths with historical, as well as living saints, world-servers, and inspirers of humanity.

Our sense of purpose, or lack of one, shapes our worldview, as reflected in how we treat ourselves and others. Living without purpose often results in the feeling of profound emptiness. Economic struggles, too, can reduce us to cogs in a wheel or spare parts in the machinery of an industrially based society, which is extremely limiting and disquieting to sentient human beings. Shifting from material-centered to spirit-centered living portends a far more satisfying existence.

While superficial living fuels our lesser natures, meditation, prayer, and deep reflection guide us toward love, kindness, compassion, forgiveness, and our better, more angelic natures, the wise have always admonished us to direct our energy toward grander, nobler, and more humane purposes. It has been said that even our hearts and souls synchronize when we serve a higher purpose. Fulfilling our highest aspirations while serving the Heavenly uplifts the human race. As the contributors to *Ignite Your Purpose* book reveal, knowing your purpose is a vital and bountiful treasure.

Thankfully, as life advances, many yearn for a more meaningful existence beyond the constraints of the mundane. A dedicated and ignited mind unleashes a deeper inner power that propels the seeker toward expansion and awakening.

It always struck me that living without purpose is akin to resigning oneself to a life of insignificance. The wisdom of all ages and cultures has always guided us toward adopting a more meaningful existence. The centrality of this search and discovery brings comfort to earnest seekers everywhere. I know that it has for me and for many of those around me.

It may be said that purpose is intertwined with identity, that in finding one's purpose, one finds one's spirit-self. A more limiting sense of purpose can stem from one's upbringing, environment, education, or obsession with materialism. As such, many tether their purpose to the struggle for survival or to vocation or career, which is fine so long as doing so makes them happy. Those who search for something deeper, however, seek a purpose that is profoundly open-ended. Approaching life artistically or philosophically can completely transform its complexion. Finding and serving a higher, more creative, and expressive purpose has filled the void in the lives of so many people. More than two thousand years ago, Cicero said: "The purpose of civilization is to bring humankind to an enlightened and cooperative state." Likewise, to love, know, create, and fulfill—these all elevate purpose while bringing contentment and fulfillment to life. A grander and noble purpose truly can make us feel whole again in a way that enhances our abilities, as well as our often hidden and stately beauty. The mundane says that our purpose must be bigger than our complaints; the sublime tells us that the Universe is an infinite place for us to worship. The span between purposes, great and small, can truly be immeasurable.

Some say that the purpose of our existence is to become self and God-realized... an embodiment of universal love and a fully realized and enlightened human being. When your light shines so bright, when your love is so pure, when your heart is so full, and your purpose is truly clear, you will come to know why you are here. Mark Twain once said: "The two most important days of your life are the day you were born, and the day you figured out why."

We live in a time when the pursuit of purpose is not a luxury but a necessity. As technology redefines reality and the boundaries of possibility, we are faced with the greater responsibility of aligning our actions with intention. The relentless pace of change and modern living can leave us feeling adrift and disconnected from our core values and principles. This is precisely why *Ignite Your Purpose* arrives as a timely companion, reminding us that while the world may change, the quest for purpose remains.

Why is finding one's purpose in life so significant? The answer lies in the profound ripple effect it has on our world. When we align with our purpose, our actions are infused with intentionality, and our impact and influence becomes immeasurable. Purpose transcends the boundaries of the individual, creating a ripple effect that extends outwardly, touching the lives of those around us, as well as the communities and world that we live in. Whether we realize it or not, each of us possesses a thread in the intricate tapestry of humanity. When we weave that thread with a greater purpose, the result is healing, uplifting, and transformational.

Consider the following purpose-compelling thoughts: purpose exists in us because there is purpose in the Universe; only you can find your greater purpose. Finding purpose helps to complete us—were life meaningless and purposeless, we would not seek for meaning and purpose. We are always united in our highest mission and purpose—there is no nobler purpose than serving with dignity, humility, and love.

At the heart of this important book lies the exploration of finding one's purpose. This is not merely a self-help exercise; it is an expedition into life's deepest chambers and processes. The author and her team of writers navigate the topic with grace and insight, weaving together personal anecdotes, wisdom from thought leaders, and practical exercises that guide readers toward genuine self-discovery. For many, the journey to purpose is often a winding path marked by introspection, vulnerability, and a need to sometimes embrace uncertainty. Through the pages of this book, readers will encounter a roadmap, a toolkit for unveiling layers of being and for understanding the unique melody that resonates within each of us.

As you journey through *Ignite Your Purpose*, allow yourself to embrace the unknown and confront the questions that linger in the quiet depths of your heart. Let the inspired contributors to this book guide you through the labyrinth of introspection while helping you emerge on the other side, aligned to your purpose and life's fulfillment, more than ever before.

In conclusion, I commend JB Owen and her outstanding team for their dedication to exploring the profound theme of purpose within the Ignite series. *Ignite Your Purpose* is not just a book; it is an invitation… a call to action that resonates with the very essence of our humanity while shining a light on one of the most important, transformative processes in the life of every individual. As you delve into its pages, may you find inspiration, guidance, and, above all else, the energy to ignite the flame of purpose within. In that spirit, go forward in life with a smile in your heart, a song of praise upon your lips, and a purpose that fills you and those around you with contentment, joy, and love!

With Gratitude,

Doug Ivanovich

Douglas Ivanovich — United States of America
WP1 Concerts CEO & Executive Producer
American Icon Awards Executive Producer
Storm Aid Foundation, Inc. Executive Director
illusionfactory.com
in *dougivanovich*
f *doug.ivanovich*

Doug Ivanovich is a business executive, musician, and highly respected visionary, writer, and speaker on the subjects of human behavior, spiritual development, virtues, values and ethics, peace and non-violence, life and consciousness, cosmology, comparative religion and philosophy, citizen diplomacy, Earth-restoration, and clean hydrogen energy. Doug will be releasing *Like Lightning From The Heart*, the first book in his highly-anticipated *Inspirational Outpourings* series, during the fourth quarter of 2023. For information and inquiries, contact Doug at: WorldPeaceOne@yahoo.com

Lady JB Owen

LADY JB OWEN

"Your guiding purpose is always bigger than just you."

My intention is to help you know that you have a defining purpose; we all do. Many of us linger to discover our purpose or delay in finding it. Some are unsure they have a purpose, but I assure you do. When we search for our purpose, we always find it. It may take time to discover, embrace, and make it known. As you look for your guiding purpose, the purpose that leads you forward, you will see that your purpose is intertwined with who you are. Your purpose is your defining reason, your mission, your desire, and your divine assignment all wrapped up into one.

WHO IS IGNITING HUMANITY?

I know that Igniting Humanity is a big idea, a colossal step, a massive under-taking. Yet, I also know we are facing a time in our world where each and every person on the planet has to care about our future. Now more than ever, we all have to think not just about ourselves, but also about the person next to us and the one on the other side of the world. We are all interconnected whether we believe so or not. We rely on each other for food, fuel, energy, transportation, communication, global stability, and more things than we can count. We are not living in an era where we must only look after ourselves. If humanity is to prevail, the entire planet has to get to a place where we all come together for a bigger purpose; to support one another in living the life we each deserve.

Although I feel this way today, I can't say I felt so compassionate about humanity all my life. There was a time when my pink Barbie™ camper and Cabbage Patch Doll™ was the center of my universe. Like most children growing up in North America in the '70s and '80s, I had Hasbro™, Nintendo™, and Lego™ to keep me constantly busy. I wasn't worried about global deforestation or melting ice caps. The view outside my window was playing tag with my friends till sunset and selling KoolAid™ on the weekend from my cherry-red wagon. I didn't know there was a war on drugs or silent killers like diabetes, lung cancer, or AIDS. I was just living my childhood life, going to school, tap dancing on Fridays, and seeing God in church on Sundays.

When I graduated, I had stars in my eyes. I studied fashion, design, and all the beautiful ways to work with fabric and make clothes. I wanted to go to the big city, see the bright lights, and enjoy everything the world had to offer. I didn't know about the famines in Ethiopia, the genocide in Rwanda, or the families fighting for their freedom in Croatia. You could say I was in my *bubble* of backcombed hair, neon joggers, and Nike™ runners. All my friends and I cared about were the clothes we wore, the food we ate, and the music we listened to. The wars, sickness, degradation, injustices, and environmental destruction that were going on around the world seemed so far away. Those things felt distant and surreal. As if they were out of our hands and not our problems to solve.

I didn't grow up in a family with blinders on, but I also didn't grow up in a home where we looked at what was happening in the world and felt like we couldn't change it. We knew that we should care, but what could possibly be done to fix it? We accepted that it was beyond our control and not for us to change. I knew I could give money to those starving in Africa and knit mittens for the homeless in Siberia. But all of the issues going on in the world seemed far from my front door. My childhood was safe and secure, and I lived in a place where no one ever worried about being kidnapped, mutilated, or raped. People near me weren't trafficked, sold, or held hostage. I was one of the lucky ones who went to bed each night with a pillow under my head and food in my tummy. It wasn't until I became older that I realized atrocities weren't just happening overseas in other countries—mistreatment and unfairness were happening everywhere.

In my late teens and early twenties, I started seeing the world firsthand. It began with our travel club in high school, then with trips I orchestrated on my own. I chose to go on longer stints that had me eventually living for 3 years in the Dominican Republic. There, I saw poverty up close and witnessed illiteracy at its height. I spent time with people who had nothing—no shoes, no food, or clothing. I saw families with 8 children to feed, all sleeping on 1 mattress; on the floor. I ate meals with a stick, cooked on an open flame, while sitting in the dirt. Corruption, prejudice, and inequality ran rampant, and for the first time in my life, I started to care deeply. In fact, I cared so much that I felt angry. Angry that the weekend brunch at the fancy hotels could easily feed an entire village. Mad that people were allowed or not allowed to go places according to the color of their skin. Furious that jobs were contingent on your last name, or who you knew, or who you bribed. Suddenly, the people that I had grown to love were being unrightfully treated and unfairly ostracized.

When I eventually left the Dominican, I had a newfound awareness of how inhumane people were being treated and how the rest of the world didn't seem to be concerned or cared. And, when I returned home, I saw how oblivious my friends were. All they focused on was fashion, movies, make-up, and music. They, like me at one time, only worried about the moment in front of them and their immediate satisfaction. That is when life started to shift, and a great chasm began to erupt in my understanding. What was happening to people wasn't just out there, somewhere foreign. The unjustness and indifference that were unfolding were happening to all people, in all countries around the globe. Humanity was sliding. Dignity for one another didn't seem important. Fairness and freedom were just words, not actualities. The safety and serenity from my childhood were not the reality of the world. Something needed to be done.

I'll admit feelings of outrage percolated within me, but as before, I wasn't sure what I could do about it. I had awoken to the state of so many unfair situations but felt unsure as to the solutions I could make. *How could I, just one person, do anything to change what was going on in the world?* I felt both perplexed and defeated on how to end world hunger or stop sex trafficking. Global warming and animal extinction were impossible for me to improve. What could I do about all the anarchy and abuse happening to our world? I felt inept and discouraged.

It wasn't until my kids were born that I finally decided I had their future to think about. Holding them in my arms and seeing their exuberant smiles, coupled with their intense curiosity about everything around them, had me seeing life through their lens. To watch them feel joyous about a butterfly or gleeful over a mud puddle changed the cynical part of me. All the questions they asked, and their innate desire to learn had me asking new of my own. They were always optimistic and cared endlessly about everything, even the birds flying against the wind or the turtles swimming in the polluted pond. They *wanted* to hold hands with their neighbor and *share* whatever food they had. Through them, I saw the beauty of giving, caring, and acceptance. They offered forgiveness and understanding first, not last. They gave without receiving. Their wide eyes always held love. It was through their unconditional openness to everything around them and their welcoming hearts that I saw how the world was supposed to be.

I knew that if I wanted my children to have the life they deserved, I needed to do something to preserve our world. I needed to be more diligent and genuine in my intentions to make a real impact. I had to not let anything stop me from ensuring they had a wonderful future before them. But before I could do that, life delivered a few more lessons for me to learn. Divorce struck my marriage—I was a single mom facing stigma, isolation, and financial struggles. I became involved with someone who introduced me to the horrors of alcoholism. His plight with drugs and liquor opened my eyes to yet another problem the world was facing: addiction, homelessness, mental illness, and prostitution. Never before had these things been a part of my life; yet, in my desire to love him, I saw the devastation they caused. I attended his meetings, visited the addiction centers, and supported him in getting people off the streets. I wanted to help so badly, but I felt helpless to assist him and anyone else. The only thing I could do was help myself and get out.

Of course, while I was healing and expanding in my own life, Covid-19 showed up. The most heinous and unfair conditioning I had ever seen. The tactics used around the virus, the behaviors of many, and the fear that engulfed the world were frightening on another level. In such a short period, *everything changed*. The pandemic incited rallies and division. Propaganda was circulating, and inhumane conditions were rising. Suddenly, *everything* felt different. My kids were being polarized and conditioned in their thinking. Fear was engulfing them, and depression was setting in. On a global scale, suicide and domestic violence increased, and words like fatality rate, quarantine trauma, doomscrolling, and mandatory social distancing were in every conversation. When I saw the light within them dim and excitement for their future dwindle, I knew the time had come for me to take action and do *something*!

I went to the computer to Google™, "Who is igniting humanity?" An international conference in 2017 called IgniteSpeakers was the top search result. A make-up line in Belgium appeared because their ad campaign said it was *igniting the glow of the skin*. I then Googled, "What woman is igniting humanity?" There were none. Women who had gone into space, invented things, and changed slavery and voting protocols appeared, but none who were pledging to help humanity right now—today! The more I searched, the more I saw how the state of humanity was crumbling. There were articles about *humanity's fallout, warfare tearing down humanity, economic imbalance for humanity*, and *humanity on the decline,* all echoing in news clip after news clip. I went to bed angry and upset that no one was making humanity important. No woman was out there vowing to improve humanity on a bigger scale. I felt enraged that there wasn't someone in the world who wanted to ignite humanity and make the world a better place for the next generation and all the generations to come.

And that is when it happened...

At that defining moment, a profound realization enveloped me. My mission, previously latent, burst forth with fervor, reminiscent of a phoenix, ablaze and eager. I felt the urge to rise, transcend challenges, and soar to uncharted territories. My spirit was fueled by an unwavering belief and an intense passion that blazed within. Overlooking injustices or *turning a blind eye* was no longer an option. The clarity of my purpose resonated deeply within me, emphasizing my commitment to be a beacon for others. It was unmistakably evident: my role in this vast universe was to inspire, uplift, and kindle the spirits of humanity, guiding them toward a brighter destiny.

I have learned that you can not expect someone to do something that you are unwilling to do yourself. And, you can not sit and complain if you do not have a solution. I have prided myself in being an action-taker and worked hard throughout my life to create good ethics and values that helped me be tenacious and driven. At that moment, I saw how all the work I had done, all the experiences I had endured, the things I had witnessed, the feelings I suppressed, and the hardships that were placed upon me were all designed to lead to that exact place of *knowing*, with full conviction, that if I wanted to Ignite Humanity, I needed to start doing it myself.

My purpose was revealed so beautifully; *to Ignite Humanity and raise the consciousness of the planet by bringing people together in heartfelt harmony.* It wasn't fancy or lengthy, filled with big words or scientific meanings. It was simple, succinct, and most importantly, it was doable, effective, and could change the state of the planet. I knew that if I lived on purpose, I could touch the lives of others, creating a massive ripple effect. In doing that, each person I impacted would be able to impact one other person in their life. That person would ignite someone else, and it would continue indefinitely. By igniting people, I could ensure that they would ignite each other. Those people could then use their talents and gifts to save the environment and reverse oppression. They could use their knowledge to find solutions to racism and quell gender discrimination. Each person I uplifted would feel inspired to uplift their friend, colleague, or neighbor. Now, we could end wars, obliterate segregation, abolish prejudice, and heal the hearts of many. By showing love, offering support, and leading with kindness, I could be a part of bringing people together, creating deeper connections that would yield forth compassion and foster communication. New opinions could be *formed*. A new vision for the future could be *birthed*.

A new awareness of what is possible could *live* in the minds of everyone. A new *hope* for the future and a greater understanding of all of humanity could be instilled in every one of us!

As I delightfully vibrated with the powerful positive energy of this purpose, I knew it was bigger than anything I could have ever decided on my own. God, a Higher Power, the Universe, and Greater Intelligence were all a part of this knowing being shown to me. The time had come to not just see the world like a bystander watching it all unfold but to make a difference in the world like I was truly invested in its success. I needed to be interested in its longevity, existence, and ability to provide for my children, my grandchildren, and all the many children after that. If I wanted the world to be a great place to live, I had to make it my mission and do my part to make it exactly that.

I won't say igniting humanity is an easy task. One's purpose seldom is. Every day, I ask myself, *am I doing enough? Am I making a difference? Is change truly happening?* In those moments, I go back to knowing that one person can ignite the life of one other person, and that person can positively impact another person after that. In such a beautiful chain reaction of goodness and pro-humanity sentimentality, I believe change will happen faster than we think. People will feel closer to one another and care about the fate of our future. We will stop worrying only about ourselves; instead, we will be invested in humanity on a global scale. It won't take long to ignite the world with love, compassion, and heartfelt connections; it is already happening. When every person begins to realize that we *can* create a better world and take upon us the actions and behaviors that uplift each other, that will be the wildfire that sparks massive change for the good of everyone.

As I walk the path of igniting others, I look back and see that throughout my life, my purpose has always been beside me. Some days, I knew it was there; others, it was lost in the fog that surrounded my human experience. Often it was whispering to me, knowing I was listening, until that day it shouted my name, and I was able to see it, clearly, diffidently, and right before me. I didn't need to find my purpose because it was never actually lost. I needed to find the person I had to become to live out my purpose and be the person it needed me to be.

Your purpose is your reason for being here, and it is supposed to take your entire life to execute. When your purpose is fulfilled you can exit this life with joy. I'd like to imagine myself sitting on a rocking chair, turning one hundred years old, ready to move on, knowing that I lived out and fulfilled my purpose graciously. I want that beautiful feeling of knowing I made a difference and that I am leaving this world better than when I arrived.

Finding your purpose is like pulling back the curtain or lifting the veil on the most amazing part of your life. It is awakening to that which already lives deep inside of you, waiting to be activated. Your purpose should be big, bold, and auspicious. It should require you to make it your life's work. If your purpose doesn't feel massive, that likely isn't it. A purpose is a calling, a devotion, a lifelong quest. It is so immense that it can't be contained. It will knock on your door daily, showing up in moments of need. It will sing to you from the rooftops and find you when you are crying in the pit. It's all around you, in you, and part of you. You don't need to find it, for it is never lost. All you need to do is muster the strength within you and *become* it. Your purpose is right there inside of you. Living your life and fulfilling your unique purpose is what the world is eagerly waiting for.

IGNITE ACTION STEPS

We all have a purpose designed to intertwine and intersect with those with whom we align and have a similar intent. Seek out those people, find them, and come together to make a difference. You are not supposed to do your purpose alone. Many are out there to join you, support you, and have the same purpose in mind. Connect with and co-create with them. Let your united force and laser focus move mountains and change policies. Allow your similar convictions to give you strength when hardships present themself, and obstacles prevail—aligning with people who share your passion and value your perseverance. They will bring you great solace, abundant grace, and the magical feeling of lifelong unity.

Know your purpose is yours. Don't try to adopt someone else's purpose— live your own. Discover it inside of you, awaken to its gift. Be of the mindset that you are your purpose and that your purpose is you. Purpose is about becoming the version of you that you were designed to become. Bask in that purpose. Love it with all your might. Learn all you can about it, and when you know that you *know*—your purpose will be the most important thing you will ever discover about yourself.

JB Owen — Canada
Speaker, Author, Publisher, CEO of Ignite, JBO Global Inc. & Lotus Liners
www.jbowen.website
www.igniteyou.life
www.lotusliners.com
jbowen
LadyJBOwen

Kjirsten Sigmund

KJIRSTEN SIGMUND

"Give your soul a chance to shape your life."

You may have spent most of your life feeling lost or directionless, only to discover that in the depths of your being lies a powerful source of wisdom and enlightenment. The path of self-discovery can be frightening and over-whelming, but it also presents us with immense opportunities for growth and transformation. You are an aspect of the Source and powerful beyond measure. Therefore, I urge you to ask, *"What if my purpose is to wake up and realize that I am God?"*

UNLOCKING GOD'S POTENTIAL

I stood on stage before my fellow actors as the air conditioner hummed a nearly meditative *Om* behind me. I closed my eyes and took myself back; to my grade 1 classroom filled with colorful posters of the ABCs and small children sitting eagerly, ready to learn. That day, my grandmother arrived early to pick me up and take me home. I asked her throughout the drive whether there was some surprise waiting for me, but she stayed silent. At age 6, I couldn't imagine what might be behind this sudden change to my schedule, but as the minutes passed without eye contact, I could sense something was wrong. When I arrived home, I was welcomed by police officers, doctors, and family friends as I sat on the long gray couch in our house. The air in the living room somehow seemed thin and dense at the same time. Then my mom's red, puffy eyes met my confused and innocent stare as she asked me, "Do you remember the angel books that we read?" That question was followed by the news that my dad had gone to join those angels.

I opened my eyes and poured the sadness and surrealness of that moment into delivering my lines. This is what it took to pursue my lifelong dream of becoming an actor. I joined one of the best schools in the country, the Lee Strasberg Theatre and Film Institute in Los Angeles. The school practices the Method Acting technique, encouraging actors to explore their emotions to create realistic and naturalistic performances. This technique challenges individuals to find motivation for their characters, drawing upon personal experiences and memories as well as imagination. I had that in spades. At the time, I thought it would be an excellent opportunity to heal some of the areas of my past that still needed transformation. But I had initiated that transformation before arriving in the big city.

Before going to LA, I had decided to move home to Vancouver Island for the summer. About 3 weeks before I was going to pack up my truck and leave for the city of angels, I woke up in the middle of the night to a lightning bolt of energy coursing through my body. My mind and thought process seemed to go offline instantly, and for a brief moment in time (which seemed like hours), I couldn't tell you who I was, what I was, where I was, what year it was, or anything that I used to consider important. All I heard was a woman's voice that said, "YES!" As I tried to catch my breath and return to reality, I wondered what she meant by "YES!" *What was she referring to? Who was this powerful voice that had just entered my whole being, rendering me to a surrendered state, to this pure transformative energy and her words? Was this my higher Self speaking to me directly?* I wondered. Little did I know that discovering the answers to those questions would take every ounce of me.

At the time, I was unclear about what was happening, although I later realized that that was the beginning of me Spiritually waking up and coming off the wheel of samsara. The wheel of samsara, also known as the cycle of rebirth or reincarnation, is a concept in Buddhism that describes the continuous cycle of life, death, and rebirth that living beings experience in accordance with their karma. It is a metaphor for the cycle of suffering that living beings endure and emphasizes the importance of understanding our actions and striving to improve them. In Buddhism, this process of breaking free is known as enlightenment, nirvana, or liberation. I was stepping into that realm in life cautiously.

I knew something was coming my way after hearing the profound voice saying YES. It was my initial crash course into learning how to listen to Spirit, as if a seal had been broken open and I had been initiated for the first time in my life. I later understood through years of sitting with Master Teachers that spiritual seals are meant to be broken open. They unlock the power of transformation and connection within each of us, allowing us to access deeper aspects of our being. When we break through these seals, we enter into a higher level of consciousness and understanding. This is where true inner growth occurs as we explore our potential for personal growth and healing. Breaking open the spiritual seals is an essential step on the path to enlightenment. It requires us to take a leap of faith and trust in ourselves, our intuition, and the unknown.

Of course, at twenty-one, trust in oneself can be hard to come by. At that stage in my journey, I was in pretty rough shape physically, mentally, emotionally, and spiritually. I was experiencing deep bouts of depression and anguish, and my inner life seemed chaotic, while my outer life seemed bland. I was frightened by the desire just to be. The physical discomfort, the depression, and the confusing emotional state were all tied up in the past. I didn't know where to start. I had finished my Undergraduate degree in Human Kinetics, and my identity was completely wrapped up in my accomplishments. However, I seemingly felt like I hadn't achieved anything of real value yet. Instead of feeling like I had achieved great things, I was feeling stuck and unclear about what my purpose indeed was. I had no explanation for the turmoil that was going on inside of me. No one, least of all myself, could explain why I felt so lost and confused. I was supposed to be having the time of my life. I was at one of the world's most famous acting schools in one of the world's most famous cities. But instead of being happy, I was in an existential crisis. I had no idea who I was.

Then, one October afternoon, I drove down to the beach. I didn't have a particular intention in going there but sensed I needed to go where the water was. As I stood there overlooking the Santa Monica cliffs and ocean, the waves crashing onto the beautiful shoreline, a question I had never asked myself before strangely came out of my mouth. I had never read any major spiritual texts before. I had no basis for or guidance toward this question. Yet, at that moment, from the depths of my heart and my being, I asked the Universe:

"Who am I?"

BUZZ! The phone in my pocket broke me instantly out of my trance. On the screen was an email from my Spiritual Teacher saying, "Some interesting experiences are coming your way regarding the illusion." At first, I wasn't sure what to make of the timely message, but then out of the blue, I had what in Spiritual circles is known as a Full Kundalini Awakening. It felt like an exceptionally strong and large amount of energy rose from the base of my spine and moved up my back, activating every chakra system in my body with pure light and consciousness. It was like a wave that moved through me, culminating in an intense yet peaceful and blissful sensation. The experience brought profound insights into the illusory nature of reality. I suddenly understood why things were the way they were, how our perception of certain events can be distorted by our beliefs and expectations, and how we can move past these illusions to see things more clearly.

My third eye was wide open, my crown chakra was connected, and my lower chakras were rooted in the earth. I hadn't even learned what a chakra was yet: this concept in Hinduism and Buddhism refers to an energy wheel or center located at various points throughout the body. Yet I could feel them spinning. I later learned that each chakra is associated with a different energy type that influences physical and psychological functions. And I was feeling energized for the first time in forever.

As the Kundalini continued to rise, the energy, although surging through my body, eventually calmed. I could almost hear a voice from the Universe answering my question. It said: "You are not your name, you are not your job title, you are not what society expects of you, you are not your opinions, beliefs, and ideas. You are limitless potential and the life force energy that has created the entire Universe." I was instantly Awake. It was like being turned on from the inside out. Light felt like it was pouring out of my skin and eyes, and I suddenly felt connected to everything and everyone around me in a profoundly omnipotent way. It was one of those moments where time seemed to stand still as if I had been granted access to some other type of reality and dimension that I had forgotten about.

The only words I could muster were, "Oh my God... I am God! "And so is everyone else; they just don't know it yet. How could I forget this?" I wondered in the overwhelmingly silent deep recesses of my "NOW" mind. Everywhere I looked, it appeared that the people around me were like actors on the stage of

Life, only they had forgotten we were in a play and had bought into the characters they thought they were playing, their "identity." My eyes opened wider, my thoughts expanded outward even further, and I felt connected to everything and everyone seemingly in a flash. I had discovered the Soul, the mysterious and ethereal part of us that resides in our very core. It's the intangible part of what makes us unique, gives us passion and purpose, and connects each one of us to something larger than ourselves. I had forgotten its power and its presence in my life as "The Soul."

Yet, it was here with me all along, that familiar spark inside my chest that glowed brighter in moments of joy and dulled during times of hardship, that spark that kept me going despite the obstacles life threw my way. That was my Soul, which had been guiding me all along, showing me the way forward with its infinite uncommon wisdom and guidance. I knew it was trying to tell me something important: that our souls are always there for us, no matter what. Even in times of darkness and despair, our Souls remain with us, reminding us of the beauty that exists from within. No matter where life takes me from here, I will never forget the power of my Soul.

Today, I understand that we live within the mystery of the soul, the mystery of life, and the mystery of divine inspiration. We are all here to be awakened by the Divine, even if it takes years for this to happen. It is our choice and free will how we go about it. *How do we use our time?* That is the next question that we must answer as we are here to awaken our souls and follow the higher path. Upon these truths, we arrive at a deeper understanding of who we are. We are not just bodies in the physical world. Our bodies may have physical forms, but they are not the true Self, just as our mind is not the authentic Self, just as our ideas are not the authentic Self. Our true Self is eternal; eternal in its life-and-death-free-will existence. Our bodies may decay away, as has happened to all human beings. Our minds may also cease to be. What we call the mind is simply an illusion. The soul and the body may be mortal, but the authentic Self has no mortal body. It is eternal, and it has always been that way.

The role of the Soul should be the object of our love, attention, and devotion. Our soul is simply the life force, the essential nature of all living beings, the Universe, and the Self. The purpose of our lives is to be our eternal expression of self, to be like the Buddha and all great spiritual masters who loved and devoted themselves to their service and others, never for fame or fortune. Their purpose was that they simply wanted to serve the world with their gifts.

In the end, I believe that the search for inner purpose is something that has been a part of the human experience for centuries. Although most people might confuse inner purpose with passion, I believe our purpose goes way beyond that. To me, purpose is an all-encompassing spiritual experience that deepens our sense of existence and gives us a greater understanding of who we are. When we live in line with our purpose, we experience spiritual liberation—a sense of freedom and fulfillment only from being aligned with our soul's essence. I have come to learn that the journey of spiritual awakening is often an unexpected one.

I, like many people in this world, have struggled to find purpose, meaning, and value at times. We often define ourselves by our jobs, relationships, or possessions. But what if our purpose goes far beyond that? What if our true purpose is to awaken to the realization that we *are* God? And to go be it in the world of time and space, serving others along the way.

The concept of 'I am God, Source, the Creator' is a way of looking at our innate spiritual nature and understanding our profound connection with the Universe. To begin, the idea of 'I am God' is not new, and it has been present throughout different cultures and traditions. Hinduism believes that the ultimate reality is Brahman, the highest form of the Divine. And Christians believe that Christ is within us, and we are all blessed with the Holy Spirit. And in secularism, the concept of unity consciousness is based on the belief that we are all interconnected and, therefore, one with the Universe. In all these perspectives, there is a common thread, and that is the idea of oneness, God's Consciousness. The oneness view entails that every living being is a manifestation of the Creator. Each of us has a Divine spark from the Creator within us, and therefore, we are capable of immense love, creativity, and spirituality. This viewpoint eliminates the idea of separation, which can lead to judgment, morality, and criticism. When we are conscious of our unity with God and the Universe, we start to love and accept ourselves as we are. We begin to realize that we are not separate from anything or anyone, making us more compassionate, open-minded, and tolerant.

The concept of oneness can also lead to a profound spiritual awakening, which it did for me. It is a realization that you are not just a physical body but a spiritual entity. This understanding will move you beyond the limitations of the physical realm and allow you to connect with the divine. It can help you release limiting beliefs and habits that have held you back and instead encourage you to become a more loving, wise, and powerful being. By understanding that you are God, you can open up to new possibilities you were not previously aware were available in your experience.

I, just like you, am connected to something greater than myself, and the Soul will carry us through any obstacle, no matter the size. We each have a unique Soul, which is the source of our creativity, resilience, and courage. Our Soul, also known as an aspect of God, has been with us since the beginning of time; it is not limited to any one thing or place but instead radiates out into the world around us. It is our job to nurture this power within ourselves so that we can live our fullest life.

When you realize that you are God, you realize that you have infinite potential to create, heal, and transform your life and the world around you. You also realize that you are responsible for your life and your experiences. You free yourself from the victim mentality and take charge of your destiny. You start living with purpose, clarity, and gratitude. You live in a state of abundance rather than scarcity. You become more loving, compassionate, and kind towards yourself and others. Whether you understand God as a divine entity or an infinite consciousness, realizing that you are part of this ultimate reality can awaken your inner wisdom, power, and love. After I woke up and realized my connection to the Divine, everything in my life began to change. I started studying with the most awakened mystics, healers, and Teachers on the planet to learn and understand more about higher consciousness and universal love and intelligence. This process gave me a deeper understanding of self-realization, the power to change your life, and how everything can be interconnected to the Source. This path has led me to become what I call an "Uncommon Wisdom" Teacher, where I help enable others to reach their highest potential in life and find the path to true Self Liberation... My teachings are centered around helping people find the courage to live in an enlightened state and see themselves as powerful spiritual beings.

Awakening to your purpose as the realization that you are God is not something you can achieve by reading a book or attending a seminar. It's an inner journey that requires a committed and consistent practice of self-reflection, meditation, and mindfulness. You start by questioning your beliefs, thoughts, emotions, and behaviors in order to learn to observe them rather than identify with them. This will support you in understanding when you can release the ego of its influence on your own thoughts, feelings, and decisions. This is an important step in embracing the present moment. The more you practice, the more awareness and clarity you gain, and the closer you get to the realization that you are God. By questioning your beliefs, thoughts, emotions, and behaviors, you begin to explore how to awaken to your purpose. You must learn to observe these experiences without judgment and let them go. They are not you, and you are not them.

I've learned that self-realization, or enlightenment, is a journey of self-discovery and growth—one that takes us beyond our limited perception of reality to an understanding of the oneness of all life. It's a process that allows us to connect with our true purpose and create a life filled with joy, love, and peace. As I've walked this path, I have understood the interconnectedness of all life and how we are part of a greater whole. I've also learned to recognize our Divine nature and realize that nothing is more powerful than living in alignment with our higher self. Ultimately, self-realization brings us closer to experiencing oneness with God. It is through this connection that we can know true love, joy, abundance, and peace that surpasses all understanding.

Life is a journey of personal growth, as well as an act of collective transformation. As we each become more attuned to our divine nature and tap into the power that lies within, we create ripples of positive change in the world around us. We can use this newfound wisdom to help make a difference in people's lives by inspiring and uplifting those around us. We can also use it to help bring about a more compassionate, just, and equitable world—a world in which everyone is treated with respect and dignity.

Self-realization is the ultimate path of spiritual growth. It's not something that happens overnight, but with practice and dedication, we can all experience its transformational power. As we open our hearts and minds to the possibilities of this journey, we can unlock the abundance that lies within and live a life of purpose.

Self-realization *is* about realizing your true potential—the power that lies within you—and using the divine, conscious wisdom to create a better world for yourself and others.

IGNITE ACTION STEPS

- Be honest and vulnerable with yourself. Ask yourself, "Who am I?" and "What do I believe?" By understanding your beliefs and thoughts, you can identify any limiting patterns that may be blocking your true purpose.

- Accept that the realization that you are God arrives in its own timing, and often in the moment when you have fully surrendered to the Divine and the awareness that you are nothing known by the mind. Your nature's truth is love.

- It is important to remember that in order to bring true harmony simul-taneously to the mind, body, and spirit, it is necessary to tend to the energy of the chakras. To restore balance to the chakras, various healing practices such as yoga, meditation, and Reiki can be used. Additionally, dietary changes, therapeutic massage, or energy healing modalities may help bring the body back into balance.

Kjirsten Sigmund — Canada
Speaker, Author, Teacher, Thought Leader, CEO of Global Life Wellness and
Uncommon Wisdom
www.globallifewellness.com
www.UncommonWisdom.com
🅕 *UncommonWisdomConsulting*
📷 *kjirstensigmund*

Yeliz Ruzgar

YELIZ RUZGAR

"Nothing is a coincidence; everything and everyone is a sign guiding you toward your life's purpose."

I wish for you to awaken the MANA (Life Force) within, and to help you discover your life's purpose and achieve inner peace. We bear a unique destiny, often obscured by material entanglements and conditioned teachings. May this story remind you that nothing is a coincidence in your life and that everything is a sign for you to become the best version of you. May it support you in your journey of self-realization and understanding your purpose in life. Now, more than ever, the world awaits the ignition of *you*.

NOTHING'S A COINCIDENCE. THIS IS A SIGN.

Little streams of light broke through the early morning darkness as the sun began to rise at St. John's Health Center in Santa Monica. The warm rays hit my eyes, but somehow felt so far away as I looked at them from my window. Above me, the white lights of the hospital room had a cold, bluish hue, and I felt like I was stuck in a dark space. As I lay on the emergency room bed, hazy from the painful night I had gone through, I heard the urgent voices of 6 doctors who surrounded me.

"She has a massive, grapefruit-sized, bleeding cyst. In rare cases, this can cause death," said one of them. As I was told I needed immediate surgery, I felt confusion, fear, and uncertainty join the pain in my abdomen, like a double punch to the stomach. As an immigrant in a foreign country with no family nearby and financial uncertainty looming over me, I felt utterly overwhelmed. I had never been hospitalized before or gone through an operation. I did not know what to do. I wanted to cry and was desperate for a hand I could hold.

This is when an unexpected visitor, *Purpose*, knocked on my door. Amidst the chaos, a voice within whispered: "Let's heal this together and help others heal from within."

Before that moment in the hospital, I had unconsciously been trying to heal myself in a very different and unhealthy way. In the depths of my loneliness and the haze of uncertainty, I found solace in excessive drinking and smoking, seeking a fleeting escape from my inner turmoil. My days were blurred by this self-imposed fog, and I yearned for something more but didn't know yet how to answer that yearning.

There was a quiet voice that was leading me toward true healing. As I made my way through each preparatory procedure, the voice got stronger. I understood it was telling me there was another way that I could heal myself from within. The doctors returned to get my consent for surgery, earnestly believing it would save my life. With gratitude but conviction in my voice, I told them, "No."

After some discussion, I finally convinced them to let me leave the hospital. In those first hours of daylight, I put pen to paper, signing what felt like an epic tome of hospital forms. Emerging from that medical realm, I was accompanied by my loyal, whispering friend, *Purpose*, a silent witness to my decision.

It was time for me to take the wheel. Literally.

I have always loved driving: the sense of control, the mind-clearing peace that comes with choosing the scenery you will take in, and being open to the journey ahead of you. As I drove down Robertson Boulevard, a long, straight road through the heart of Los Angeles, I began to cry. That cry became an uncontrolled sob, as a sense of helplessness and desperation overtook me. I needed to know where I was supposed to go next and what to pin my hopes on. The pouring rain obscured my view through the windshield as my tears blurred my vision of everything around me. I cried out to God, "Please show me a sign! Please show me that everything will be okay, that I am guided and protected."

In the blurry mess, I could only see a bright red sign with bold yellow letters. It read, "Nothing is a coincidence. This is a sign."

Wow! I asked for a sign and, "boom!" there it was. I pulled over the car immediately to investigate the sign further and discovered it was hung on a large building, above a huge wooden door carved with Eastern designs. As I knocked, I did not know what to expect. I was greeted by a woman who told me it was a special day for their spiritual center, and they were having a private celebration. I was getting ready to turn away when she told me, "I don't think it's a coincidence you found us on this day. Your spiritual birthday is today."

Many years later, a numerological reading would confirm that prediction was true… that the destined day of my spiritual birth was precisely the day I followed the sign and found that spiritual center.

The following Tuesday, when I returned to that building, I was invited to join a group and handed a book. A spiritual guide told us, "Today, we will be learning about this ancient spiritual book written in Aramaic, the language of the prophets." As I looked down at the cover, I immediately flashed back to age thirteen, seeing the same book in my hand as I crossed the Aegean Sea on a boat from my home city in Izmir, Turkey, half a world away. I have been guided toward the wisdom in this book from a young age. *Nothing is a coincidence.*

As I learned from these ancient texts and these Kabbalah masters, I felt a shift within me. For all the uncertainties surrounding my life, I felt an inner guidance that my purpose lay ahead if I simply followed the path I was being shown. Their teachings were joined by the whispers of my loyal friend, Purpose.

I began to contemplate how to bring love, peace, and healing to myself, with the inner knowing it would help me bring it to others. Stepping onto the path of self-healing was far from easy; it was a leap of faith into the unknown, a daring commitment to embrace transformation through lifestyle changes. I summoned the courage to bid farewell to my job and the life that had grown stale over time. For more than 4 months, I sought refuge in the nurturing cocoon of my nurse friend's haven, a sanctuary primed for healing.

In the gentle cadence of those days, I rewrote the script of my existence. The slow rhythm of life itself became my guide, leading me toward newfound perspectives. Shedding disempowering beliefs and embracing a mindset of resilience, I embarked on a journey of self-discovery. Nourishing my body with wholesome choices, I immersed myself in the timeless wisdom of Ayurveda and Macrobiotics. Yoga and meditation wove their way into my daily routine, each pose and breath a step closer to inner tranquility.

However, my transformation didn't halt there. During the subsequent phase of my journey, a powerful wave of empowerment surged within me, breathing vitality into my spirit. Exploring the teachings of Huna, the ancient Hawaiian Spiritual Practice, illuminated my path further. I unearthed the profound truth that realigning with my soul's purpose revitalized the very essence of life within me. Sunrises became moments of gentle awakening, and gratitude painted every facet of my existence.

That feeling was so serene... the very essence of the deepest inner peace. All I wanted was to share this feeling with others. This is where Purpose went from a constant whisper to a statement of bold conviction.

As purpose led me, I dared to venture beyond the confines of the corporate world, a leap fueled by my inner calling to live a life *on* purpose. That led me to establish my holistic coaching and consulting business in the heart of Southern California. The fledgling days were not without their challenges, but in the company of fellow healers and holistic health practitioners, a grand idea took root. Collaborating with one of my customers, we birthed something transformative—a series of yoga and health festivals across 10 cities in the United States, honoring the art of healing the body, an initiative we called National Yoga Month. The ripple effect of our vision was astounding. In 2008, a significant milestone was reached when the USA Department of Health and Wellness officially proclaimed September as National Yoga Month. From then on, September became a time of celebration, a collective honoring of the profound impact yoga and holistic health have on our lives.

As the years unfolded, my journey gathered momentum, propelled by courage and unwavering commitment to Purpose, who had knocked on my hospital door all those years ago. But it wasn't until 2010, at the transformative event named *Date with Destiny*, led by Anthony Robbins, that my purpose evolved even further.

There I was, at JW Marriott Palm Springs, where Tony was holding his destiny-altering event. We had just emerged from a oneness-deeksha blessing, an experience that left me breathless and in a state of heightened awareness. I felt the energy coursing through me, the connection to something beyond myself. Then everything slowed down; time seemed to stop, and I could feel nothing but the faint throb of my own pulse in my hands. The world around me became silent as if a veil had been drawn over reality. In that stillness, a voice began to speak.

"Your reason for being, your purpose of life, is creation, transformation, and exploring your potential. It is just you and I on this physical plane, and no one else. Everyone you meet is a part of you. They are you, and you are

them. Until you learn to love each and every person you encounter, until you gather all the soul sparks and lessons from others, your transformation will continue. Love is the key to transforming 'me' into 'we,' and ultimately into divinity. Your highest potential is all that exists. Your purpose is to awaken yourself each year to a better version of you."

This was the culmination of a journey that had led me to become one with all that there is. As I stood in that room, surrounded by the electric energy, I felt a profound shift within me. It was as if a shroud had lifted, revealing a reality beyond the surface of things. My whole being was suffused with love, a love that transcended words and boundaries. In that moment, love wasn't just an emotion; it was a force, a vibration that pulsed through every cell of my being. I was like a beacon of light, radiating this love outward, touching everything around me. I was no longer just an individual. I was connected to the Universe, a part of a grand tapestry of existence. It was a feeling of oneness, of unity with all of creation. Time itself seemed to fade away, and I was enveloped in the mystic realm of the *"Now."* There was no before, no after; there was only this present moment, and it was suffused with an indescribable peace. The worries of the past and the uncertainties of the future melted away, leaving only the serenity of the present.

As I basked in this state of bliss, a thought floated into my consciousness. It was a simple thought, yet it carried profound implications. *We can even end wars*, it whispered, *when every person on the planet experiences this state of inner peace.* The implications of that thought resonated deeply with me. I understood that the divisions that had torn humanity apart for centuries could be healed through the power of this love, this unity of being. Imagine a world where individuals from different faiths, backgrounds, and cultures, are connected to the source of peace within themselves. Imagine a world where the barriers of prejudice and misunderstanding crumbled in the face of this shared experience of love. It was a vision of harmony.

At that moment, I saw a glimmer of what mystics had spoken of throughout history. It was a glimpse into the profound truth that when we connect with our true essence when we align with the core of our being, we can transform not only ourselves but the world around us. It was a reminder that love was the ultimate force of transformation, the key to unlocking our higher potential. As I stood there, vibrating with love and immersed in the "now," I knew that my purpose had expanded even further. It wasn't just about my personal journey of healing and transformation; it was about sharing this experience with others and helping them tap into their own wellspring of inner peace and love.

The journey was far from over, but I was fueled by a newfound clarity and conviction. Purpose, once a quiet whisper, had become a resounding call to action. I was ready to carry this message of love, unity, and transformation out into the world, to be a beacon of light in a sometimes-darkened world.

As I followed my purpose, my deepest desire to help and heal others took many shapes. I co-authored books alongside luminaries whose very names echoed greatness. I stood on stages shared by the likes of the Dalai Lama, Byron Katie, Dr. Joe Dispenza, and more holistic leaders whose presence illuminated my journey. I gave a TEDx Talk titled "Nothing is a coincidence. This is a sign," a reminder that life's synchronicities are not mere accidents, but powerful signs pointing us toward purpose and meaning. In the vast realm of the internet, my talk found its wings, soaring across digital landscapes to touch the lives of over half a million viewers.

That number is powerful, in and of itself, and proves how universal the quest for purpose is. In all my learning and exploration, I have learned that, above all, *we are not alone* as we seek the meaning behind our existence. The quest for life's purpose dates back to ancient times and has been explored across different countries and cultures. *Mana, Plan de Vida,* and *Ikigai* are just some of the terms used by various civilizations to express the concept of life's purpose. Ikigai translates to "A reason for being" or "One's reason for waking up in the morning."

There is no stronger reason to wake up, for me, than to have another day to share the deep, peaceful love I have found on my journey. I get to see the silver linings threaded between all these happenstances of my life. My courageous decision to defy standard medical practices and pursue self-healing through lifestyle changes demonstrates the transformative power of living on purpose. By aligning with my truth, I was able to overcome health challenges and thrive. Keeping this truth as my guide in my journey with Purpose led me down a deeply fulfilling and meaningful path, and allowed me to invite others to walk it. Each moment I encountered was a chance for me to reflect, grow, and find out why I was brought into this world. The journey I embarked upon was one of profound revelation, and its impact endures, as listeners and seekers unite in their shared pursuit of purpose.

Let us remember that our words, our stories, and our moments of vulnerability have the power to spark revolutions within hearts. As we embrace life's unexpected signs and synchronicities, we become conduits of inspiration and catalysts of change. We are given daily opportunities to see the signs and discover that nothing is a coincidence.

IGNITE ACTION STEPS

In history, Victor Frankl recognized that 'purpose' is vital for optimal functioning, especially during the most significant adversities. Those who survived unfathomable conditions they faced had someone or something to live for. Living with purpose positively impacts physical, mental, and emotional health, leading to overall success and longevity. Research has shown that people who live with purpose exhibit 5 common characteristics: physical well-being, psychological well-being, resilience, a positive outlook, giving back, and success and achievement. Here is how you can incorporate the steps from my accredited and award-winning Mana Life Purpose and Wellness Program to begin unlocking the purpose-driven person within you.

1. **Physical Well-being—Commit to the Sunrise Routine**
   For the next twenty-one days, commit to waking up at sunrise. This routine can provide a fresh start to your day and create a conducive environment for self-reflection and introspection.

2. **Psychological Well-being—Engage in Journaling**
   Over the course of these twenty-one days, dedicate a portion of each morning to journaling about the following inquiries: *What activities bring me joy? Where do my talents lie? What do others often seek my assistance with? How can I harmonize a fulfilling life that incorporates my passions while also addressing a global challenge? In essence, what truly constitutes my life's purpose?*
   Be honest and introspective while exploring your thoughts and feelings.

3. **Resilience and Positive Outlook—Reflect on Passions and Talents**
   Use journaling to deeply explore your passions and talents. Consider the things that genuinely ignite your enthusiasm and those activities or skills at which you excel. These passions and talents could be hints toward your life purpose, as they often align with what brings you joy and what you naturally excel at.

4. **Giving Back—Identify Opportunities to Contribute**
   Think about how your passions and talents could be utilized to help others and contribute to your community. Consider the organizations or causes that resonate with you and align with your values. Explore

how you can make a positive impact through volunteering, sharing your expertise, or offering your resources to these organizations.

5. **Success and Achievement—Seize the Opportunity to Act**
Once you've completed the twenty-one days of journaling and reflection, review your insights. Look for patterns, connections, and themes that emerge from your responses. Use this clarity to start crafting a plan for how you can incorporate your passions, talents, and desire to contribute to your life.

Yeliz Ruzgar — United States of America & Turkey
Speaker, Author, PhD. Lifestyle Medicine,
Founder of MANA Life Purpose & Wellness
www.manabook.club
groups/manaland
manabookofficial

IGNITE™
your
Purpose

Purpose Prompt 1

DEVELOP AN ABUNDANCE MINDSET

When you acknowledge the abundance around you and practice gratitude intentionally, you open yourself up to discovering your purpose. List 5 things you are grateful for in your life right now:

1. _____

_____

_____

2. _____

_____

_____

3. _____

_____

_____

4. _____

_____

_____

5. _____

_____

_____

Purpose Prompt 2

PURPOSE AND HAPPINESS

How does knowing your purpose make you happier?

_____

_____

_____

_____

_____

_____

_____

_____

_____

_____

_____

_____

_____

_____

_____

_____

_____

_____

Randy Dyck

RANDY DYCK

"Adversity defines not who we are, but how we rise."

My hope is when you face adversity, it gives you an extraordinary opportunity to discover the depths of your courage, resilience, and gratefulness. It acts as a crucible, refining and revealing the purest form of your character. Adversity, in its unique way, brings true clarity. It strips away all that's superficial, exposing what truly matters—your spirit, your resolve, your purpose in life, and the very essence of you.

"RETURN ON LIFE"

The quiet that surrounded me was deafening! Yet, in the distance of my subconscious, I could hear Gerry, my fourteen-year-old twin brother yelling as he stood over me. "You wrecked the motorcycle! You wrecked *our* motorcycle!" I was drifting in and out of consciousness until, in one particular conscious moment, I realized I couldn't get up. I mumbled and indicated for Gerry to help me. He reached for my left arm and began to pull me up as he had done so many other times after a fall, crash, or crazy, reckless stunt—activities befitting of 2 mischievous and curious twins on a grain farm in Southern Alberta, Canada. However, this time something in me signaled for him not to pull, but instead to go get help. Gerry put my arm down and ran.

Lying on the ground in my silence, I began putting the pieces of the puzzle together. Gerry and I were told to remove the skateboard ramp from the front driveway since we would be hosting choir guests singing in our country church. Dad wanted the ugly, eyesore ramp removed before they arrived. As we loaded the ramp into the bed of the pickup, we both agreed without a word to race to the drop-off point of the ramp. Every day… everything… became a race for the 2 of us. We were perfectly matched competitors since we were identical twins, and beating him felt like my sole purpose. My race machine was our shared motorcycle, and his race machine was the pickup truck transporting the skateboard ramp.

Racers ready! No one was around to fire the starter pistol, but we knew the race was on. Little did we know this race was *not* going to end in a victory, at least not in the short term. It all happened in a flash, but in that moment, everything seemed to play out in slow motion. *Slow is fast.* Crucible moments heighten our senses; we often see and remember things we wouldn't see or remember outside of the moment. Through a series of racing and riding errors, I torpedoed off my bike into our storage shed, helmet-less and headfirst.

Lying in the still and silence alone, I waited for help. It was all I could do since I couldn't get up. *Slow is fast.* What seemed like forever laying there alone wasn't long at all. Yet, I had time to take in and see the vibrant green spring leaves of the trees up against the deep blue May sky. Gerry had sprinted to our house, a football field away, to find my dad and older brother Rod. Getting ready for church, they were each having a shower. In an emotional and panicked voice, Gerry shouted into each bathroom, "Randy's had a bad accident and needs help!"

Slow is fast. Out of nowhere, they appeared: Dad in a bathrobe and Rod with a bath towel around his waist. Things got real. Dad kneeled down; his initial gaze was unblinking, fixed on me, the motorcycle, then back on me. Then in a concerned and passionate yet quiet and controlled voice, he asked if I could feel or move my hands and fingers. At that moment, I realized I had not moved a muscle since gaining consciousness. My arms lay on the ground beside my head as if I was a bank teller in a robbery being told to "Stick-em-up." I tried with all my might to move them, but they were frozen to the ground, and I replied to Dad with a shaky "No." Dad asked if I could move my legs. Again, "No." I could feel them, but just as heavy dead limbs.

Dad was a doer, a performer, and an individual you could count on to execute anything he took on. Dad was built for that moment. He quickly asked Rod and Gerry to get the butchering table from the shop. The 3 of them slid the butchering table under me like a modern-day backboard, carefully keeping my neck stable. Then, carefully, they began the *slow, fast* transport to the house.

Once in the garage, Dad called 911 from the garage phone, an unusual place for a phone, especially in the '70s. The call went like this: "My son has had a serious accident and has suffered a neck injury that has caused paralysis from the neck down." Hearing the word *paralysis* triggered my mind into mental gymnastics. This buzzword had been spoken around my high school over the previous 10 days. 2 individuals, one a forty-year-old man and the other a sixteen-year-old student at my school, were paralyzed in separate vehicle accidents. Theirs were 2 stories with a lot of air time in our small town and were now playing big time in my head.

Slow is NOT fast. The ambulance was taking forever to arrive. I was now going into shock, shivering cold, shaking uncontrollably, and the pain was intense. I lay on the butcher table staring at the garage ceiling, the first of many I would study in the coming months. Looking at the automatic garage door opener, all I could hear echoing in my head was the word *paralysis, paralysis, paralysis*. More mental gymnastics, silent words, and questions kept coming to the surface of my fear. I asked myself, *Will I be like the 2 other individuals in our small town that were paralyzed last week? Will I ever walk again? What will life be like in a wheelchair? Why me, God?*

Slow is fast. The ambulance finally arrived. No sirens, just lights, as we made the bumpy 5-mile gravel road trip from the farm to the hospital. Upon arriving, I was surprised at the number of onlookers assembled on the hospital's outside steps. The stairs gave a bird's eye view of the ER entrance and the patient being hauled in. It was like a red carpet entrance, but this was no party.

This is where things get fuzzy but intense. I was rolled into the ER, then the X-ray room, and then out of nowhere, my Mom appeared. I can't imagine what she was thinking as she traveled twenty-six miles from our country church to the hospital. As a father of 3 children, I now know that seeing your child hurt and in pain is so gut-wrenching that if you could, you would put yourself in their place. Even at the moment, heavily sedated with drugs, concussed, traumatized, and in shock, I could feel my mother's warmth, love, and unconditional desire to take all the pain away. And then the lights went out.

Where am I? My head feels like it is going to explode! Moan, groan, everything hurts, the intensity of pain in my neck. I hear the words *paralysis, paralysis, paralysis* again, followed by the same frightening questions in my head.

Breakfast is served. My parents, Gerry, and a doctor walked into the room. *Slow is fast*; the doctor talked about his diagnosis and next steps. But I heard nothing. Gerry heard nothing as well. He and I were having our own non-verbal conversation. In our silence, we were reaching out to each other. My extrasensory perception whispered *I am scared and afraid*; *I need your help to get me through whatever is coming my way*. In his own whisper, he shared the same; *I am scared and afraid also, together we will get through this*. Then I heard the doctor say, "We are transporting Randy to the spinal cord injury ward at Calgary Foothills Hospital," some one hundred twenty miles away. So much was coming at me, yet all I could think about was the unanswered questions about my potentially paralyzed future.

Once I was settled into the ward, an angelic-looking nurse introduced me to my new patient-mates. One was the sixteen-year-old kid from my high school who was paralyzed the week before. The room became silent; nothing was said to make the connection between him and me at that time. He had no idea who I was, but I knew who he was even before the accident because he was 2 years older than me and had a pretty cool truck. Unfortunately, it was the cool truck that now left him a paraplegic. By now, he was post-surgery, fitted for a wheelchair, and starting his new life without the use of his legs. Wow, too real. The fellow I feared I would become was in the bed across the room from me.

The first few days were really tough. The visitors were great, but they had so many questions, and so much of my energy was spent on being present with them. I just wanted to be in a quiet space with Gerry and my parents. The catheter was not fun, and because my organs had shut down from the trauma to the spinal cord, my waterworks and bowels were missing in action. The traction device was extremely painful for my jaw. It was a halter that wrapped around my neck, almost like I was being hung from a tree with a noose. But instead of a vertical hanging, it was a horizontal hanging while lying in bed with weights attached and pulling on it.

It wasn't all bad news. Within the first week of arriving at Foothills and being in traction, I was beginning to get feeling back in my legs and right arm. It was still sluggish, but I could move, feel, and use them; a huge victory. The challenge was my left arm. *Come on, wake up. You're late to the celebration.* But the best part of my early recovery stages was that the ESP whispering between Gerry and I had changed from, *I am scared and afraid*, to *We got this, and we will get through it together.* My doctor added to the encouraging messaging. He continued praising my progress and how my body was responding to the traction. My spinal cord was not severed or crushed, only scarred and traumatized, and the traction had reduced swelling, so my feeling was being restored.

He then spoke and shared something I will never forget...

"Randy, you are lucky to be alive; your fractured neck and the blow you took to your head would have killed most on the spot. *Randy, someone has much bigger plans for you."*

At that moment, he gave me the confidence to believe that one day I would be the Randy I was before my head-on torpedoing into a building. That moment ignited my inner warrior and gave me a purpose; to fight for my recovery.

Yet that warrior within would be tested almost immediately. The horizontal traction noose had been helping, but after more X-Rays, my doctor decided surgery was needed. I was devastated, scared, unsure of what to expect, and my doctor saw it all over my face. He assured me that surgery was best for me and said there were no other options. I called my Mom, and I began to sob. Another setback, more loneliness, unknowns, pain, and *Why me?*

Then Mom said softly yet confidently, "Randy, you are strong and courageous, and you will get through this. *God has a bigger plan for you."*

The next morning brought new hope. Hope is everything, and my doctor was great at delivering the good news. "Randy, the surgery went extremely well." Day thirty-nine since the start of the race that almost ended my life. *Slow is fast,* and things were progressing nicely. I was always a shrimp (skinny runt, scrawny pip-squeak... just a few names that were thrown at me as a kid in the schoolyard and sports fields). But I took it to a new level. The scale barely tipped sixty pounds, and I was very frail. Yet, I was filled with hope, gratitude, and joy. I still couldn't walk more than fifty feet without lying down and resting. A small half-pound weight felt like one hundred pounds, but hope was in the room again. More importantly, my competitive juices were coming alive in a big way, reminding me of my former purpose.

What got me into this mess was competitive juices, but it was also what was going to help me become whole again. The same nature that made me race Gerry to our toy box, the bus stop, and the skate ramp was about to become my superpower.

Unexpectedly, my older brother, Rod, visited me on day forty-six. And unexpectedly, I was told I was ready to go home—even more unexpectedly, I was afraid to leave. The hospital had become my home and my security blanket. The surroundings, nurses, the routine, the smells and odors, the yucky food, and even how I could keep my emotions in check were all a comfort in their own ways. Fear, anxiousness, and uncertainty filled my mind. All I knew was the world of the Hospital. Fear of returning to my old world of the farm, as a 'new me,' was messing with my safe place. Rod did his best to encourage me and explain why I should be thrilled to be leaving the hospital.

The word got out that I was being discharged, and I had a parade of nurses swing by to say their goodbyes. Rod gathered the few things I had into a shoe box. He loaded me into the front passenger seat, and we were off for the one hundred twenty-mile trip to the farm. It was a beautiful June day. The sun shone, the windows rolled down, and I was dying. My neck, back, and bum hurt, and even my eyes hurt from the vibrant non-hospital colors. Everything hurt!

Slow is fast. The drive went fast, even in my pain state. I overcame my fear of leaving the hospital and was thrilled to see the farm and be home with my family and, more importantly, my twin brother. Oh my goodness, the view was spectacular. We lived on a large hill we called hurricane hump because of the strong west winds that would blow in Southern Alberta. But that day, there wasn't a breath of wind and the spring crop that Dad had planted was a deep lush green. The view overlooking the Valley and the town of Pincher Creek with the amazing Rocky Mountains in the background was stunning—home sweet home.

The process of home recovery and physical rebuilding was to begin. I left Foothills Hospital with no physio plan. I didn't think much of it at the moment, but in hindsight, it didn't make sense. I guess God had a better recovery and physio plan for me. It was called being a competitive twin. Gerry and I were neck and neck before the accident in everything we did (no pun intended): basketball, motorcycle racing, hockey, running, boxing, skiing, and even checkers. Anything we did, we were equals until now. I was disabled, frail, and trying to get a lazy, limp, weak left arm and hand to work again. But if I had learned anything over the past forty-six days, it was: *that I was here for a purpose beyond what I thought. I faced adversity in the eye and discovered the depths of my courage, resilience, and gratefulness.*

Racers ready! Over the next year, Gerry pushed, supported, and raced with me to help me become his equal competitor again. Slow *is* fast! Playing sports, running, riding the same motorcycle again, and giving me wins when he could easily beat me. He was my everything: support, confidant, brother, and hero for the journey of adversity. He inspired me to be great again and helped me find my purpose.

As I reflect on that life-altering day forty-five years ago, the profound lessons it instilled have become the cornerstone of my journey as a father, a businessman, and simply a human being. The accident wasn't a setback, but a setup for understanding the deeper layers of life. It became the starting line for a victorious life filled with purpose. I have been privileged to illuminate the paths of many, helping them understand their unique purpose and harness life's adversities as stepping stones to their greatness. In going through challenges, purpose unfolds in ways that reveal the larger meaning of who we are and who we become. *Slow is fast.* Be patient because purpose shows up when you least expect and need it most.

Racers ready! When you are positioned to run a life race filled with purpose, you have to be the one to fire the starter pistol. *Adversity defines not who we are, but how we rise.*

IGNITE ACTION STEPS

- **Discover Yourself:** Confront your adversities and perceive them not as roadblocks, but as opportunities to uncover your true purpose. They can be crucial moments that help to reveal the path you're meant to follow.

- **Cultivate Gratitude:** Amid the difficulties, find the silver lining that directs you to your purpose. Cherish the learnings and personal growth that adversity brings, and remain grateful for how these challenges shape your journey toward your purpose.

- **Engage in Reflection:** Adversity is a crucible for your character and purpose. Reflect on your experiences during those trying times. Learn from them, and refine your purpose. Use those insights to align your actions and decisions with your overarching purpose.

Randy Dyck — Canada
Speaker, Author, Entrepreneur, Podcaster, Coach,
Adventure-seeker, Adrenaline-junkie
www.randydyck.com
randy.dyck.98
randycdyck

Kanika Rose Raney

KANIKA ROSE RANEY

*"We are all in charge of creating a life that allows us
to live in our purpose, on our terms."*

The sweetest rewards in life come from living in your purpose, but doing so can sometimes take you outside the boundaries of your comfort zone. If the thought of being true to your purpose evokes fear in you, it is my hope that my story releases you from whatever is holding you back. I want you to see that your purpose gives you power; finding comfort in knowing your purpose serves as a compass when you don't know where to go or what to do. Embrace the awareness that your purpose gives you permission to be bold and live the life you were meant to live.

KALEIDOSCOPE

In my mind, I could see myself walking to the edge of the cliff. Standing there, I could feel the breeze of promise on my face, my nose breathing in the smell of the sweet success, and my heart embracing the dreams of my ancestors. I raised my arms so I could look through the kaleidoscope once more to see the beautiful colors, mesmerizing patterns, and intricate shapes rotating section by section, with each turn representing the steps of my career. I could also feel the cold, shiny metal rubbing against my wrist and a slight pinch of tightness on my skin. Despite the physical discomfort, I couldn't help but find emotional comfort in the familiar. Having worn them for so long, these golden handcuffs gave me a sense of security. This luminous set of linked metal rings represented a multi-6-figure salary, 6-figure bonuses, stock options, and other alluring financial trappings. And it wasn't just about the money. These golden handcuffs glistened with power, prestige, and access. The irony is these things that made me feel secure were actually designed to secure me from the very thing I needed to break free from.

Even though it was imaginary, standing at the edge of that cliff was frightening. I found myself teetering there many times, but fear, comfort, and society's expectations kept me from taking the leap and pursuing my true purpose. Ironically, if you asked my closest friends to describe me, they would likely start out by saying I'm bold, followed by outgoing, sharp-witted, skillful, stylish, and unexpectedly comical. They would also be very quick to say I live life on my own terms—"Kanika is not afraid to put herself out there, whether it's through her straightforward way of engaging with others or being undaunted in the face of challenges and the unknown."

In the workplace, I'm known for my authenticity, candor, advocacy, and ability to inspire those around me. If you asked me how I would describe myself, the first words that would come to mind are introverted, empathic, intentional, and focused. What some describe as outgoing, I view myself as a friendly person who enjoys the company of others, that is, until my energy is zapped and I need to go off on my own to recharge. As an empath, in addition to my own feelings, I feel the emotions of others deeply; therefore, I'm quick to call out the unjust, advocate for equity, and support the marginalized. While others may see me as a fearless risk taker, I view myself as someone who practices 'calculated adventurism.' Yes, I've made some audacious moves, like giving up a full scholarship, quitting dental school with no backup plan for my life or career, and starting a career in an industry I knew nothing about. I also chose to have a child, wasn't married, and moved with my 2-year-old son 3 thousand miles away from friends and family to start a new job. But, these decisions were all made through intention, prayer, and careful planning.

The real question is, who is Kanika Rose Raney? Other than a woman who bears the same middle name as her maternal grandmother, I am all of the things my friends and colleagues see in me and who I believe I am. I am also a child of God, daughter, mother, sister, aunt, Godmother, sorority sister, and friend to many whose paths I've crossed throughout my life experiences. I am passionate about making good things great, being the voice of the voiceless, making extraordinary connections, and helping others navigate career success. My personal mission is *Connect. Inspire. Empower. Ensure everyone gets a seat at the table, has a voice, and is heard.* Who I am has led me to be wildly successful, gain access to unique opportunities, and benefit from exclusive experiences. Despite success and certain privileges, some barriers and distractions prevented me from doing what truly mattered. What was most important to me were the things that aligned with my values and beliefs, a.k.a. my purpose.

My drive to succeed started early. I grew up with 2 parents who both went to college and had master's degrees and long careers in their respective fields. They were the children of parents who also went to college. When I was growing up, I would follow suit: graduate from high school, go to college, then maybe medical or law school, or even get a good-paying job in Corporate America, climbing that ladder as high as I could. I wouldn't be relegated to certain jobs like my parents were. My father was a Pastor, and my mother was a teacher, 2 jobs offering many opportunities for educated Black Americans in the 1960s. To branch out and get that good-paying corporate job meant I'd made it. It meant that all the sacrifices made for my generation were now producing the desired impact.

No one ever dared to push me to explore going into business for myself. I saw others doing it but never saw it as an option for me. Outside of having a medical or law practice, entrepreneurship was for those who couldn't make it in the corporate world. It worked for those with a partner or spouse who could provide stability and benefits. You started your own business if you didn't want to deal with corporate politics. Negative stereotypes such as entrepreneurs being money-motivated, egotistical, and unable to work with others made me believe it was for someone other than me. I was meant to align myself with a corporation with strong values, work with others, follow the rules, play it safe, and climb the corporate ladder. In fact, as a child, I envisioned myself wearing suits with a briefcase, going into a giant office building every day.

That childhood 'suits & briefcases' dream eventually led to a frustrating reality. I don't like to think of myself as a statistic, but the findings from a study conducted by Leanin.org and McKinsey & Company reveal a distressing truth, one that I, unfortunately, know all too well. One that kept me coming back to the edge of the proverbial cliff time and time again, only to turn around and have those shiny handcuffs placed back on me once again, thinking, *This time will be different.*

According to the *Women in the Workplace Report*, 49% of Black women in America feel that their race or ethnicity will make it harder for them to get a raise, promotion, or chance to get ahead, compared to just 3% of white women and 11% of women overall. As a Black woman working in Corporate America over the past twenty-five years, I've lived this exhausting reality—experiencing the mental, physical, and emotional toll. In fact, I've often felt like I was living in a real-life kaleidoscope. It's a world made up of different shapes, colors, and patterns, all of which are constantly moving, with complex sequences, being represented in infinite ways. The shapes that emerged in the kaleidoscope symbolize the "rules of engagement," or what I realized were unwritten rules of which I was completely ignorant as a first-generation entrant to the world of global Fortune 500 companies. The colors of the kaleidoscope embody the culture of the organizations I've worked in. From company to company, each corporate culture was unique. What was *not* unique was the feeling of *not* belonging. The patterns in the kaleidoscope depict the systemic barriers and biases that show up in the workplace, no matter where I turn.

I experienced and witnessed others who look like me endure blatant discrimination in the form of unfair and inconsistent hiring and promotion practices, pay inequity, and being overlooked for development programs and stretch assignments. Then there was the multitude of microaggressions, those indirect, subtle, or unintentional actions that can create a hostile or uncomfortable work environment for members of marginalized groups. This challenged the notion of being able to pursue my purpose in Corporate America.

Imagine someone saying, "You don't sound [Insert your race here]," or the one comment I find particularly triggering every time it's said to me, directly or about another Black, Asian, or Hispanic person, "You are so articulate." What do they expect from someone who grew up in America, has a college degree, and successfully made it through the same interview process they did? I've heard, "You're different from the others." Colleagues have also called me by other people's names, which was typically the name of the only other Black woman in the organization. Once, I had a colleague say to me, "I went to the beach the entire weekend, and look, I'm almost as dark as you!" I've also witnessed Black colleagues have their identity questioned because of the texture of their hair or the lightness of their skin. They've had to endure endless questions about their hairstyles and have often had to play "duck and dodge" to avoid having colleagues touch their hair. Personal space, please? These are just a few comments and experiences I've endured and witnessed throughout my career.

I've often been in meetings as the only Black person or the only woman, having my ideas ignored or dismissed, only to hear someone from the dominant culture present them later and get praise. I've had non-Black colleagues tell me that they don't see color. *Does that mean they don't see me?* I've seen leaders deny Asians and Hispanics promotions in the workplace because they were 'too quiet' despite their exemplary performance and stellar impact.

As a Black woman, I live at the intersectionality of my race *and* gender. As a female, I'm expected to be nice, agreeable, and nurturing. However, when exhibited by a woman, typical leadership competencies needed to advance in corporate America, like being assertive, candid, competitive, decisive, and having high-performance expectations of my team, are interpreted as being aggressive, scary, or too demanding. As a woman, when I push for advancement or higher pay, I'm seen as being pushy or expecting too much, while my white male counterparts are perceived as "go-getters" for the same behavior. I'm expected to be grateful, always engage humbly and stay in my rightful place as a Black woman. Trying to navigate a culture that was created by and for white men created a continuous feeling of exclusion, uncertainty, and unworthiness. All of this kept pushing me closer to the cliff. Just when I'd thought there was a recognizable pattern in the kaleidoscope, with familiar shapes and colors, the sequence would change

Despite the above statistics and experiences, I've been extremely blessed to have a thriving career, working for some of America's most beloved and influential companies, quickly progressing as a leader in global roles, exponentially increasing my impact, income, and success. I believed my work was aligned with my purpose, but I still felt stifled and limited in how much change I could impart in the areas where I had the most passion. I take responsibility and find joy in advocating for fairness and equity, especially for women and people of color. My own experiences and being a witness to those of other marginalized communities ignited a fire within me, compelling me to want to make a difference and invest in those who often went unnoticed, were devalued, and left underutilized.

I found that as I continued to move up in my career, it became more difficult to advocate for the things that were important to me in a meaningful way. Occasionally, I would consider shedding myself of those golden handcuffs. You see, I always had a key, and sometimes, I would boldly grab the key and confidently take steps to set myself free. But, I learned that intention without purpose is futile.

To feed my desire to connect with people on a different level and foster my own autonomy, I dabbled in the art of the side hustle. I started a business selling beauty products and did quite well at it. I enjoyed the independence, flexibility, and rewards. I did not like how the sales process made me feel like I was alienating family and friends or how product inventory took over my home. I lost confidence in what I was selling, became disengaged, and eventually walked away from being an independent contractor with this global network marketing company. There was a time that a close friend and I had the idea to start a business that would focus on promoting self-love and confidence in women. We created a business name, had a catchy slogan, and started doing workshops. But we eventually lost sight of our purpose in this space and got sucked back into focusing on our corporate jobs.

At one point in my career, I had been laid off, and I was enjoying some time to myself before jumping back into the corporate grind. However, during that time, I had some consultancy work fall into my lap, so I formed an LLC, and just like that, I was an entrepreneur again. It wasn't purpose-driven work or a situation created with intention, so it's no surprise that this was yet another brief venture. It was easy to step away because I was presented with an amazing opportunity back in the corporate jungle — the kind that makes you move to places you said you'd never move to, gives your family and friends bragging rights, and creates the foundation for generational wealth, all the while snapping those golden handcuffs right back on your wrists.

After dabbling in entrepreneurship without intention, I convinced myself that Corporate America was the holy grail. In my eyes, it was all a part of moving up in the world, meeting my family's expectations, and keeping up with the pace of my brilliant ladder-climbing friends. Being in Human Resources, I saw up close how white men maneuvered in the corporate realm and found success on their terms. Through keen observation and well-intentioned mentors, I learned the rules of Corporate America, both the written and unwritten ones. I knew that if I played by the rules, I would continue to excel in my career and be able to enjoy the trappings of large global companies and all that came with it.

As a Black woman, I experienced unfulfilled promises, chased moving goalposts, and saw carrots continue to get dangled in front of me. As a Black woman, I felt expectations were higher for me than my white counterparts. It also seemed like I was forced to work 10 times as hard and demonstrate significantly more impact than those around me who didn't look like me. I had to prove myself and fight for opportunities continuously that I knew I was already qualified for, which I was worthy of.

After 25 years of what used to look like confusing shapes, colors, and patterns, had become mesmerizing designs, elaborate systems that I knew how to decipher. My sense of security numbed my wrists, making the golden handcuffs feel comfortable. I no longer felt the metal pinching and scraping against my skin. Still, I did feel trapped. As an Aquarius, who values her freedom, this is my worst nightmare. I found this to be especially true since, through it all, my purpose continued to burn inside of me like a fire. I couldn't help but wonder, how do I break free of this shiny metal contraption wrapped around my wrists? As lovely and alluring as these handcuffs were, I knew there had to be something more.

Like every year in my career, it was time for my year-end performance review. These meetings typically resulted in me receiving a highly favorable evaluation, with praise for my achievements and impact from the prior year. Given what I had accomplished, I expected that this year would be no different. I walked in, confident and excited about what was to come. That excitement was short-lived. I received a performance rating that I knew was not commensurate with the competencies I demonstrated and the results and impact I had achieved. I was also passed over for a promotion I knew I deserved.

A wave of emotions surged through me like a tempestuous storm. Anger burned within me, its flames licking at my insides. I could feel the intensity of my frustration sitting heavy on my chest, and each breath became a laborious struggle against the invisible burden of inequity. Disappointment settled upon my shoulders like a weighted blanket, bearing down upon me with an unrelenting force. My limbs felt heavy, burdened with the hypocrisy of unfulfilled expectations set up by the system. My heart felt as if it had been clenched in an iron grip, slowly constricting, denying it the oxygen of hope and promise it so desperately sought.

It was at that moment that those gold handcuffs seemed to lose their luster, as if a dark shadow had descended, veiling everything in a melancholic haze. The once-familiar patterns, shapes, and colors of the kaleidoscope became distorted, edges blurred by the tears of anger that threatened to spill from my eyes. The hurt carved deep into the core of my being, piercing through layers of self-assurance and leaving behind raw, tender wounds. As I stood there, lost in a sea of emotions, all I could do was take a deep breath, swallow the bitter taste of what felt like defeat, and steel myself for the journey ahead. Standing there on the ledge, once again, taking it all in, I knew I had a decision to make. I could choose the comfortable, familiar path or I could *Ignite My Purpose*.

I chose to redefine my reality. I decided to create a reality that allows me to live in my purpose. June 19, 2023 was my last day in corporate America. This was also Juneteenth, a federal holiday in the United States commemorating the emancipation of enslaved African Americans. Was this a coincidence? *No.* This was me taking intentional action, creating freedom, embracing choice, and building my legacy. I walked up to the edge of the cliff and this time I did not turn around. I decided to stop waiting for someone to give me something that I could give to myself. I promoted myself and became the Founder and CEO of my company, *Thrive Ever After™*. It's my game, my field and I play by my rules.

For I know that my purpose lies in facilitating transformation of people and organizations. I work with companies and institutions to shift culture, mindsets and behaviors to create inclusive and equitable work environments. I help women and people of color experience a rich and fulfilling life by unleashing their power to live & work authentically, with intention, purpose and ease. Will I ever go back to corporate life? Maybe. What I can say with certainty is right now the best way I can create impact through my purpose is by choosing entrepreneurship.

Those golden handcuffs were real. The kaleidoscope was real. That cliff was real. After living in this reality for twenty-five years, I got to my breaking point. As the American voting and civil rights activist, Fannie Lou Hammer said, "I'm sick and tired of being sick and tired." As I stood firm with no bungee, tall and with my head held high, I contemplated transitioning to my new reality. Inhale courage. Exhale fear. Inhale freedom. Exhale bondage. Inhale confidence. Exhale limiting beliefs. I knew right then and there that I had only one choice to make. Remove the golden handcuffs, take the leap, and trust that I will fly.

Living in my purpose wouldn't have happened unless I was willing. It was a choice. Now when I look through the lens of the kaleidoscope, where I used to see chaos, I see shapes with perfect angles and symmetry symbolizing balance and harmony. The beautiful colors and unique patterns represent opportunity, change, and growth. I am no longer shackled, living a life in which the uncomfortable became comfortable. I choose to live a life empowered by my purpose, one that puts me at the forefront of helping others to tap into their innate power and thrive in life and business. If I don't know anything else, I know for sure that we are all in charge of creating a life that allows us to live in our purpose on our terms.

When you're living in your purpose, you should feel like you're in a state of flow. It should not feel like you're standing on the edge of a cliff, afraid to jump. You won't be paralyzed. You won't be in an endless loop of indecision. It shouldn't feel like tight constraints around your wrist or a kaleidoscope with senseless shapes, colors, and patterns. Purpose is rooted in intention, and it gives you the audacity to choose you. When you get to this place, you may feel some anxiety. With that, I challenge you to consider whether what you're feeling is indeed anxiousness, which is an emotion grounded in fear and resistance. Or are you excited, an emotion that is associated with joy, curiosity, and openness? If what you are doing is truly aligned with your purpose, what you're feeling *is* excitement, possibility, hope, and a future that God has been waiting to open up to you.

Ignite Action Steps

Are you ready to release your fear and unleash your purpose? Then THRIVE is for you!

T: Tune into your strengths and what brings you joy so you can operate in your *Zone of Genius*. Complete CliftonStrengths assessment to identify and understand your strengths. Read *The Big Leap: Conquer Your Hidden Fear and Take Life to the Next Level* by Gay Hendricks.

H: Honor yourself by setting healthy boundaries and practicing self-care regularly. Know what you're willing to say yes to, and be clear about the things you will say no to. Don't forget to enforce the boundary. Define what self-care means for you and prioritize those things.

R - Release limiting beliefs. Recognize and release any fears, doubts, or limiting beliefs that hold you back. Challenge negative thoughts and replace them with empowering beliefs; Find a mantra, scripture, or affirmation that empowers you to push beyond your boundaries. One of my favorites is from the Bible, Ephesians 2:10, *Rest in the fact that God has given you everything you need.*

I: Intentional action. Declare a big hairy audacious goal (BHAG) that aligns with your purpose, and then break down this BHAG into smaller actionable tasks. Develop a plan of action and commit to taking consistent and purposeful steps toward your BHAGs.

V: Visualize success. Create a vivid mental image of what success looks like for you. Visualize the positive outcomes and impact that living with purpose will bring.

E: Engage with a supportive community. Build your circle of influence with like-minded individuals who are aligned with your vision and will encourage you to live in alignment with your purpose. Surround yourself with those who have taken similar leaps of faith and can provide guidance and motivation along your journey. Ask for help. Help others.

Kanika Rose Raney — United States of America
Speaker, Consultant, Coach, Founder and CEO of Thrive Ever After(TM)
www.thriveeverafter.com
kanika@thriveeverafter.com
kanika.raney
kanikaraney
kanikaroseraney

Purpose Prompt 3

RECOGNIZE YOUR PROGRESS

Everything you do, no matter how small, is important and noteworthy. Write down 3 things you've done that you are proud of.

1. _____

_____

_____

_____

2. _____

_____

_____

_____

3. _____

_____

_____

_____

_____

What are the commonalities in these three things?

_____

_____

_____

How do they align with your purpose?

_____

_____

_____

_____

_____

_____

_____

_____

_____

_____

_____

_____

K.R. Rosser

K.R. ROSSER

"Purpose is the spark within you that illuminates the trail of possibilities."

My greatest desire is for you, the reader, to not just find your purpose but light it on fire. I hope my journey to understand my purpose ignites your inner drive and empowers you to live your life on purpose. May this book serve as a spark, kindling the flame of purpose within you, lighting a trail of inspiration for you and others to follow.

TOUR OF DUTY

I made it past the last security checkpoint and I knew in order to make my flight I had to sprint. Carrying my briefcase and a purse I ran until I finally got to my gate. I shouted, "I'm here! I'm here!" as the flight attendant called last call. She looked at me and said, "Are you Karen?" I nodded my head. "We have been looking for you, you just made it." I smiled in gratitude. She scanned my boarding pass and I walked rapidly down the jet way, trying to catch my breath. As I entered the plane, the last person to board, I received a resounding round of applause and cheers. Someone shouted, "Finally you made it, we can take off now."

Feeling embarrassed, I put my head down and as I made my way to my seat still trying to catch my breath. I quickly threw my briefcase in the overhead bin and plopped down in my seat near the window. I buckled my seatbelt and closed my eyes as I tried to regain my composure. The passenger in the seat next to me asked me if I was okay. I said, "Yes, just trying to catch my breath, I almost missed this flight."

I wasn't just breathless from running. I was also straight up scared. I had never traveled internationally before and as we began our taxi to the runway for take off, fear came over me. I began to realize I was headed to Germany where I didn't know anyone and couldn't speak the language. I had a sponsor but had no idea who he was or how he looked. The plane started its ascent into the sky and off we went to Europe. Oh my goodness I could not turn back now.

I engaged in small talk with the passenger in the seat next to me. He was very pleasant. I shared with him that I was in the military and I was headed to my first duty station. He said, "Thank you for your service." I nodded with a smile and responded thank you in return. This simple chat with a kind stranger was a nice way to break up all the nervous chaos in my mind.

I stared out the window for some time in a sort of trance, my thoughts swaying between disbelief and anxious excitement before all that gave way to sheer exhaustion. I asked my seat mate if he would wake me if I fell asleep when the meals and snacks were being served. I slipped off my shoes and got comfortable. I looked at the clouds until my eyes closed and I drifted off into a sound sleep. It seemed like a short time before I was awakened by a light tap on my shoulder from my neighbor, telling me snacks were being served. I sat up straight, let my tray table down, and waited patiently for the flight attendants to get to my row. I could use a drink and a snack to put my mind at ease.

Once I made my selection, I started to play a crossword puzzle and then found a good movie to watch. I started to gaze out the window again, thinking to myself, *Where did I ever get this strength to be bold and brave?* I thought about the foreign place that I was moving to and what it would be like. I wondered how the people would be and how the food would taste. After a few minutes my eyes began to flutter and off to sleep I went again. I woke to silence and darkness in the cabin. I gazed out the window again and saw the blackness of the night. The only light I saw was the blinking red on the plane's wings. My mind began to drift into thoughts about other things I had no control over: *When would my car arrive, and my household goods? Where would I live and how would I interact with the people in Germany when I didn't know the language?* Then I thought to myself, *Why did my life's path take such a dramatic turn? Was this really what I was supposed to be doing?*

The day I was born, my purpose on this earth had already been written and etched in stone. But I didn't know that. It would take a journey into a foreign land before I realized that my life had a purpose and I needed to embrace it.

I didn't know my purpose yet, but I did think a lot about the job I was taking on. The thought of me being in charge and leading Soldiers scared me to death. I was going to be in charge of someone else's son, daughter, sibling, husband and wife. Who would have ever thought this was the path I would take? I didn't go to college to join the military, I went to get a degree and become a dentist. Now I was blazing a trail toward something new, and it was terrifying. I wondered, *how I would fit in, whether they would like me and follow my orders, whether I knew what I was doing, and if I would ever go to war.* All of these thoughts ran through my mind and weighed heavily on me.

Off in the distance I could see the horizon began to get lighter as the plane continued on its path to Europe. Then suddenly, the cabin lights came on and it was time for breakfast. After a few short hours the announcement came over the intercom system that the flight attendants would make one last trip through the aisle to pick up any trash as we started our descent into Rhein Main Airport in Frankfurt. *Oh geez. Oh here we go.*

The nerves were all I could feel now, as we deplaned and I followed the crowd toward customs. I didn't want to draw any unnecessary attention to myself because I felt lost. I was standing in the baggage claim area waiting for my bags when a taller gentleman with a lean physique and short hair approached me. He said "Are you Karen?" I hesitated for a moment then said, "Yes I am." He reached his hand out and said "I'm your sponsor." I felt a sense of ease and sighed with relief. My sponsor was here to greet me, so I was safe. We gathered my bags, loaded them into his car and off we went to my hotel. We made a stop for dinner and I enjoyed schnitzel and pomme frites for the first time. It was delicious; something I could eat each and every day.

After arriving at my hotel, I tried my best to stay awake to adjust to the new time zone. Well that didn't last long at all. After showering I turned on the TV and it took no time for me to collapse into a deep sleep. I would wake in the early morning and it felt like I had been sleeping for fifteen hours but I had only slept a few. I wouldn't sleep much after that as I kept checking the clock, afraid to oversleep and miss my ride in the morning. It would take me nearly a month before my body and sleep schedule adjusted to this new time zone.

After half a day of in-processing into my new unit I was ready to get to work. I had on my semi-shined boots and freshly pressed uniform adorned with my gold Second Lieutenant bars that were glistening in the sun. I felt good, and if

I do say so myself, I was looking like a lean and mean fighting machine. After an introduction to my Commander and First Sergeant, I headed to the Tactical Site where I would be working alongside most of the Soldiers.

That lean and mean feeling faded quick. I had butterflies in my stomach and thought to myself, *What have I really gotten myself into?* I walked on the site, filled with intimidating equipment, and was met with stares from the Soldiers. It almost made me want to pinch myself to make sure this was real. As I walked around and said hello, my nerves began to get the best of me. I had to step outside and take a few deep breaths. It felt like all eyes were on the newbie, and those eyes made me feel really uncomfortable. *Maybe I don't belong here. Maybe they don't want me here.* I was being checked out from head to toe and I could see a few people whispering. Normally, I would have asked, "What's all the chatter and whispering about?" but I kept my cool and continued to smile. I wondered, *Is something wrong with my uniform? Or is it just because I am the new girl in the unit, fresh out of training?*

Something in me was sure that there was a reason I had come to Germany. Therefore, I took a deep breath and moved forward with the assignment I had been given. Over the next several months, I tried to learn as much as I could about the organization, policies, the people and the weapon system. I was required to certify as a Tactical Control Officer within my first 90 days, which only added to the uneasy feeling as I tried to settle in. There was a lot for me to learn and the train was moving fast so I had to jump right in and keep trucking. I tested once and failed after second guessing myself and missing just one question. I was devastated and my confidence was shaken, but I had no time to dwell on it. I remembered my grandmother had told me, "You can do anything if you put your mind to it." So, back to studying I went. A few weeks later I would retest and receive my certification. Finally I was on my way and could now pull my 24 hour duty like the other officers in the organization. I was ready to focus on leading my platoon and making them the best in the organization.

My day-to-day routine over the next three years was simple. Early morning physical training, accountability formation, working on the Tactical Site all day and attending meetings and field exercises. It didn't take long before I started to really nestle in with my platoon and engage in getting to know the members who I served with each day. I had some of America's finest sons and daughters in my platoon and they ensured that I was taken care of. I was provided a boot shining class by one of the enlisted Soldiers who kindly told me that my boot shine was horrible. Another enlisted Soldier told me that I should leave work late so that he could teach me all of the aspects of the weapon system and reporting procedures. To each request I obliged, I had nothing to lose but everything to gain. I was having fun and learning so much from the members of my platoon. I felt a sense of belonging; like we were family.

My purpose for being there, at that time, in that place, was beginning to blossom. I would be a source of good will and encouragement and lead with distinction in every way possible. My Soldiers and I would talk about almost anything and most would come to me seeking advice about personal matters or career choices. It felt good to know that the Soldiers valued my opinion and would talk openly with me about their issues. I would always say, "Do you want the politically correct answer, or do you want the Karen Rosser version?" I welcomed feedback and valued the opinions and thoughts of others. I believed it made them feel significant and that they belonged. And in my platoon, they *did* belong. I knew without them, I didn't have a team. Although the rank structure meant everyone had their place, I looked at us as being equals. I valued them each as a person and I never made anyone feel "less than." I wouldn't ask anyone to do something I wouldn't do. During weekly maintenance I would be right there with my Soldiers cleaning my weapon and my vehicle. During training exercises, I would assist with running cables to get the system set up and operational. Their work was my work.

However, not all times were good. There were times when I had to be stern and instill punishment. Just like a parent teaching their child a valuable lesson, punishing them was heartbreaking for me. But it had to be done to ensure good order and discipline within the ranks. I wanted to provide counsel to members of my platoon for unsatisfactory behavior, and ensure they understood they could recover. We would get through these rough times and still remain a unified, cohesive team.

That team came through for me in a big way, and helped me discover my purpose. My first night pulling a 24-hour shift with a small crew started off quiet. But in the early morning hours, I was surprised with an on-site evaluation from the headquarters evaluation team. No Tactical Control Officer wants to face the evaluation team right at the end of a shift, when the crews are about to change over. These evaluators would come to your site at any given time and see if you were prepared to fire a missile within a designated time frame. That particular morning, I had just finished my system checks and my crew was relaxing. The blare of the siren startled me. I almost made it through my shift, and suddenly it was showtime. My heart was pounding, and the nerves I'd felt when I first arrived in Germany came back with a vengeance. *Oh geez. Oh here we go.* I gave the orders, and my crew followed them to a tee, but the evaluator was taking all kinds of notes and watching his pen scratching that paper had me worried.

When it was time for the out brief, my stomach was in a knot. But my Soldiers weren't worried at all; and they were right not to be. In that high pressure surprise test, we performed so well that the evaluators were floored. There were high fives all around as I felt the lean and mean fighting machine coming back and standing tall. The late nights I stayed on site to learn the system definitely paid off. From then on my crew and I had bragging rights and from that point we never failed an evaluation. I had finally proven to myself I was an asset to the team, and there was a purpose for this newbie's tour of duty; that purpose which was written the day I was born.

I let go of any self-doubt or fears and led with a purpose. I knew I was right where I was supposed to be in life at that time. I was in this organization to inspire others, motivate them to thrive and grow. Everytime I felt like I wanted to throw in the towel and end my military career, I reflected on how many lives I touched and how many lives touched mine. I thought about how accepting of me Soldiers were, how passionate they were about their jobs, and the many conversations we had about life, family and careers. Some of them really admired me and were happy to have a female leader in a male dominant organization. I was someone they could definitely relate to. I was on my way to defining myself and I understood that my purpose transcended beyond mere duty. *It had always been about me serving something greater than myself.*

I would spend three years in that organization and serve in other leadership positions and different platoons. I was leading from the front; empowering others to do better and reach for their highest potential. My platoon encouraged and inspired me daily which allowed me to delve into the many dimensions of purpose, that inspired my life with a meaning and new direction. I was guiding my team *with* purpose, living my life *on* purpose and *feeling* purposeful. I finally understood that joining the military and being assigned to an overseas assignment for my first duty station wasn't about the location or the assignment itself. It was about self-discovery, growth, and serving. It'was about the profound effect on those who touched my life as well as the lives I touched in return. To this day, I carry those lessons with me in all that I do.

Today, the confidence and skills I perfected through military leadership are used daily in my second career as a Program Manager. I often reflect back to my first platoon when I was presented with challenges in life that seem overwhelming. I can hear them whispering, "Ma'am you got this, keep pushing," and I manage to make it through. I often chuckle at myself when I think about my first day at my unit, the second lieutenant who was scared to death — the gal with the dull boots and a big smile who managed to impact so many lives. If I had to do this all over again, I wouldn't change a thing.

Purpose is the light that empowers *you* to find joy and satisfaction in *your* life's journey. Everyone has potential that they may not realize. I always tell people to explore opportunities beyond their reach. Be bold and live life to the fullest. Take a leap of faith and believe in yourself. The only thing that is standing between *you* and finding *your* purpose is YOU!

As you take the steps and embark upon your journey, you may ask yourself, *What is the purpose of this?* If you continue to ignite the fire within you, leading *with* purpose and living *on* purpose, it won't be long before the answer reveals itself and illuminates the trails of possibilities that only YOU will blaze.

IGNITE ACTION STEPS

- **There is a purpose for everything that occurs in your life.** Recognize that finding your purpose is not done in a few minutes/seconds, it is an ongoing process that requires patience, change and willingness to make adjustments as you journey throughout life.

- **Self Reflection, Discovery, and Exploration.** Surround yourself with people that encourage you, support you, and help you along the way while you are in search of your purpose and on your personal seeking journey.

- **Meditate to gain clarity and inner peace.** Celebrate achievements on your journey to find your purpose by fostering a purposeful mindset. Set achievable goals, deadlines and remain accountable. Evaluate how your life aligns with your purpose.

- **Live your life on purpose.** Let it be a guiding light and ignite it on fire by creating a brighter and purposeful future.

Karen R. Rosser — United States of America
Best Selling Author, Former Senior Army Officer, Acquisition Professional
⊙ notsoshy_town

Xila C. Hope

XILA C. HOPE
MS, MBATM, DCPM

"PUSH the limits to break the barriers!"

We are in a time when people are casually saying, "You're on mute," as a signal for someone to resolve a technological concern. Meanwhile, there are people who are experiencing neurological deficits causing their own mental muteness, and we are not signaling them to talk. Additionally, when people are sharing, we are often unconsciously muting them ourselves. We all have the power to speak up and advocate for those without a voice, but I hope you are encouraged to embrace your own mute button. We can achieve healthier dialogues when others have the opportunity to speak.

PIERCE THE SILENCE

It was the end of the day and all of the children were running around the classroom. As I entered, I reached for my son's jacket from his cubby, but suddenly blood was rushing from between my legs like running water from a faucet. I was in a red puddle, also in shock about what just occurred. I was equally concerned that I may have created a traumatic experience for a group of toddlers who were simply excited to go home.

Fortunately, the teacher quickly moved the children to another classroom and then came to my aid, though she was just as confused about the circumstances. In the aftermath, we contacted my husband and a close friend who could arrive immediately. While I was praying for God's healing, I remembered that earlier in the day my body signaled to me that something wasn't right. Although I called my doctor, his staff didn't sense any urgency. They silenced the concerns I tried to voice. Indeed, this was disappointing because, as a black woman in America, there is a constant normalization that our healthcare concerns are dismissed during maternity care which leads to adverse outcomes.

I had recently given birth to my third child with no major complications. My previous two birth experiences had been extremely difficult, so my husband was understandably worried by this turn of events. He rushed me to urgent care. I can recall being asked many questions by the on-call doctor, and it seemed like she didn't want to deal with a postpartum patient. Although I knew I needed help, my words were falling on deaf ears, and I began to feel like it was a total waste of time being there.

I remember laying on the bed, looking up at the bare ceiling, praying to God, letting Him know He couldn't take me out just yet! I was able to silently say, *I haven't achieved my purpose.* In the midst of the pain I was feeling, something else began to happen. I felt my body going limp. I told my husband he had to find the staff immediately. The nurse entered the room and quickly called for the doctor who arrived and told the nurse to get an IV. The doctor then asked if I had taken any medication while in the room. I responded no. I was asked the same question again, in a different manner, and gave the same response! My blood pressure had dropped drastically, and they needed to correct it right away. *Did she not hear me during intake when I said I had just suddenly lost a lot of blood?* You know what? It made sense. At my arrival, I was not actively bleeding so the information I shared was obviously dismissed. Again, my voice was not heard.

While feeling like my body was finally in recovery mode, it awakened my thoughts about my purpose in life. I had another conversation, but this time with myself. I said, "What would my granny tell someone about me?" First, I chuckled, because she says some crazy things! For instance, she'll tell you, "Xila can talk someone down from a hotel to a three-room apartment." *What does this even mean?* Or she'll say, "She's a damn loudmouth! You betta not tell her what she can't do. And, if you have something of hers, you betta GIVE it up!" Being that my granny is the one person that knows me very well, I can only decipher her messaging to mean that I am a challenger and can be outspoken. I will cause you to question things that are casually mentioned with no logical sense. Lastly, I am the type of person to change circumstances to benefit us all.

Therefore, it was befitting that laying on that hospital bed was where I discovered my purpose. I knew that God gave me special gifts, even if someone spoke of them in a hurtful or comical manner. These gifts I had been given were amplification, understanding, courage, and leadership, which directly aligned with the sayings of my granny. Moreover, it was breathtaking to know that biblical scriptures also supported my life engagements since I raised my voice to speak what is right so that we don't suffer in silence. When people needed help and lacked the voice to get the results, I was there to advocate and be their bullhorn. I've also witnessed those who choose to be muted (thinking it was the easiest course of action) and recognized people who experienced a physiological or neurological reaction that caused them to mute instantly. Therefore, it's no mistake that God positioned me to strategically interrupt the silence.

Although I entered the hospital at risk of becoming a statistic of the maternal mortality rate, I left stronger than ever. There I realized I was meant to be a social activist because my granny spoke life over my purpose to anyone who would listen. That gave me the strength to support the muted person in finding their voice and reaching their full potential. My recollection of being a 'loudmouth' has always been to simply have the courage to say what was not being said. I can best illustrate this with the parenting of my own children. Each one has some form of limitation with their ability to communicate. Although different opinions were stated about their cognitive functioning, God made no mistake when He appointed me to raise them from a level of muteness to vocalization. He also made me strong enough to play the 'game' and equipped me to win. Even when that game was Charades!

Charades was what we called it at first. When my daughter was at the age where other children were beginning to speak, she would motion her body parts to indicate what she was trying to verbalize because she was determined to be heard. Over time, I also observed my daughter's frustration with people failing to comprehend her amid her various communication deficiencies. My mother said, "*Chile'*, she is doing charades." Eventually, I learned that my daughter was autistic and had apraxia of speech. She became my one child to *push* me to learn aspects of sign language to ensure there was no barrier to meeting her needs. Little did she know I had a history with this language. I started a petition while I was in high school to have sign language as an official option for students to meet foreign language requirements for graduation.

I remember sitting in our division and being instructed to select a foreign language to take. I think the only options presented were Spanish and French. At the time, I thought, *Why?* In fact, some of my very own peers were deaf. So, it only made sense to have sign language as an additional option. I did a small survey with those who were of hearing and with an interpreter of the hearing impaired. Everyone thought it was a great idea and said they would support my petition. I took the next steps to get signatures so that I could present the information to the school's Principal.

In my mind as a young person, I was very hopeful that the Principal would approve the request. It checked the boxes! It would (1) foster inclusion for the entire student body; (2) establish some behavior norms; (3) create opportunities, such as being able to serve that community when they had an immediate need; and (4) the students could have simple conversations with this population, plus have a skill set for the rest of their life. Imagine how the hearing impaired would have felt to be socially included with this one act of thoughtfulness. They would have finally been heard by someone who may have otherwise ignored their presence.

Unfortunately, my hopefulness went sailing! One day, out of the blue, the assistant principal got wind of the petition and snatched it right out of my hands as we transitioned between classes. I distinctly recall how he said I had no approval and balled the petition up in my face. While I tried to plead my case on the spot, he turned his back on me and made his way back to his office. I felt like I was watching my voice disappear down the hallway, and I had no one to speak up in my defense.

A school hallway would be the very place where my oldest son lost his desire to speak up and use his voice. It was a voice that he barely utilized, known as the gentle giant of few words. He had been instructed to go see an administrator but turned away in opposition. As he walked down the hallway, he was choke-slammed to the ground by a staff member and sustained other injuries to multiple parts of his body. When he arrived home, my heart was crushed to pieces. I had not even received notification from anyone at the school. The next day my pain suddenly went deeper, like being stabbed in the chest, when I saw the video footage with the principal. It confirmed who my son was—not one to intentionally cause trouble and who avoided confrontation. To witness my child being abused by an authority figure angered my soul and triggered many tears. But, I knew I needed to determine my next course of action and speak up with a greater purpose.

I did whatever I could to get him justice, but no one listened to my appeal. Those in positions of power consciously chose to ignore what I had to say. I surely needed an attorney at the time, but I could only afford a consultation, which resulted in the sheriff not even serving this individual. We never had our voices heard in front of a judge. Considering the totality of everything, I think this factored into my son's perception of interfacing with adults. He preferred not to talk to them.

The severeness of his struggles to speak carried into his first year of college. I was told by a senior-level staff member that they wished he *would just find his voice*. This brought tears to my eyes because I knew he could communicate.

His voice was in his written language, already an author with so much to say. I wondered, *Could he be experiencing selective mutism?* I worked hard to try to get him to surface his voice despite prior rejections he'd experienced. I would give him the words to say and encourage him to talk to people; coaching him through the script to try to make him comfortable. Also, as any parent would do, if he got into trouble, I expected him to understand his actions or inactions. I made him write out explanations of what occurred and why he had made his choices. I was at my wit's end to use anything to get him to express himself more and speak up. Unfortunately, the muteness prevented him from even engaging in healthy discussions, causing me to have to speak up on his behalf.

However, he *pushed* me to fall back from being his mouthpiece so that he could access a mic (and one that had the mute button disabled)! As the mother of this adult child and athlete, I realize it is necessary to disengage on the front end. I am in pursuit of him growing his wings to gain experience speaking his own words and conceptualizing situations. Otherwise, he will use me as his barrier when faced with hardship or good fortune. Hearing an adult man say, "My momma said…," or, "Please go talk to my mom," makes me cringe. Therefore, it is important that I help him improve his communication channels in order to establish personal accountability for his affairs and be an example to his younger brother, who watches his every move and soaks it in like a sponge.

His younger brother, fourteen years his junior; my middle child is the most talkative one. He can go onto any basketball court and play like he's been in training all his life. No fear. No intimidation. He watched his brother so much that, as a lefty, he followed through with his right hand, very contrary to the norms of the sport. As a talker, he ended up with the nickname *Dip*. He was so alert to everything surrounding him and would dip into your conversation just as if he was one of the main participants. But, there's a speech disfluency that causes him to stutter. Sometimes his delay is mistaken as a period when it is just a pause. There are many times when I have to interject to tell people *he's not finished; let him get it out*! Fortunately, his engagement in conversations was almost like the disfluency didn't exist. I truly admire his traits because he is what the Bible tells us. He sets an example despite being young and aspires always to excel.

However, during his initial years as a school-aged child, he started to go mute. Our talks decreased whenever he was distressed. It seemed like his entire body would go numb. I couldn't understand it, which made me want to speak out in annoyance. I would feel my chest inflating with a fire to discover what was at the root of his silence, what issue could be keeping him from expressing himself. This was my child who didn't miss a beat because he wanted to be included and wanted you to have every little detail. It disturbed me that there was nothing I could do to get him out of his silent episode. For the first time in my life, I had no words to help. He *pushed* me to be creative.

I decided to give him a platform to talk openly. He became the host of *The Dip Show!* As a junior chef, he communicates to his peers (and some adults who find his humor entertaining) about the cooking process. I was determined to ensure that he wouldn't continue to lose his voice like his big brother had. Working on the show allowed him to be who God called him to be, while I explored information with the medical and educational professionals.

For the majority of my life, I have been engaging with professionals who had the expertise to transform situations that I was closely connected to as an advocate. Despite the emotional hurdles I endured, especially with my own children, it was always my desire to see different outcomes. As a mother, I cried and got mad, but truly my energy had to be placed on how I could make an effective impact. Therefore, I noticed as I contributed it was always from a voice of advocacy. It was my heart that yearned for meaningful change, and it inevitably always expanded beyond the walls of my household by also giving hope to others. Simply due to the success I yielded from speaking up. I continue to PUSH barriers out of the way and drive efforts toward all voices having a place in the atmosphere and being heard at tables where decisions are being made. I do this as a social activist, particularly focusing on those with verbal limitations. This is due to the great people in my life; they positioned the use of my voice to transcend my immediate reach so that God's infinite power can show up.

God spoke and created everything into being. He didn't use His hands; He used His voice. My granny used her voice to manifest my purpose into life. Therefore, the utterance of words is powerful, and if we have been blessed with a voice, we must use it for the glory of God. He doesn't want us to be silent; He said to speak with great boldness. Through Christ, I have been strengthened to break the silence of the voiceless. While fulfilling my purpose, he blessed me with three children who each had differences in producing sounds and words. This enabled me to use my purpose to *push* limits that caused interference with their greatness. This also meant *pushing* myself out of the way or exploring alternative ways to foster communication.

We must discern when our vocalization can impart the change we wish to see for our children. Everyone needs a voice that can be heard on all channels. Your voice is your power; open your mouth and be heard. Communication, in general, allows us to connect with one another. I encourage you to recognize when there isn't balance in your dialogues and to support unique messaging channels from those you may interface with routinely or randomly. You and I can be the beacon for humanity to pierce through the silence!

Ignite Action Steps

- **Press your mute button and give up the mic!** In order to let others have their voices heard and be socially included, we have to learn to share the floor. If you're working on a team, let each person have a turn to speak and provide input.

- **Stay in pursuit despite being silenced.** God has blessed you with gifts that support why He created you! Obstacles will try to get you off course and silence you in the process. Be encouraged to discover the hope that is inherently within you. Hope gives you perseverance toward achieving your purpose.

- **Recognize the potential in the youth.** It may be your voice that needs to get in front of a story, so that the youth gain wings to fly toward their dreams. Ask them questions and listen to their answers. And, if necessary, tell them they're on mute, so that they can recognize their voice needs to be heard.

- **Be conscious of the unspoken.** Learn how to create environments where all thoughts and ideas are welcome to be voiced. Always be accommodating to those with speech and hearing deficiencies; it may cause you to pause and reflect on your normal behavior styles. If necessary, meet with those in positions of power to see what change you can support.

Xila C. Hope, MS, MBATM, DCPM — United States of America
Mother, Principal Designer and Founder of: HIS Wingspan[SM],
HER Wingspan, and The Dip Show, International Best Selling Author,
Advocate, Social Activist, a Loudmouth!
www.piercethesilence.com and www.hiswingspan.com/theshop
spreadthedip and chopetoday
spreadthedip and chopetoday
spreadthedip and chopetoday
spreadthedip and chopetoday
spreadthedip and chopetoday
chopetoday and spreadthedip

Sharni Quinn

Sharni Quinn

*"Bring more Yin to your Yang so you can stress less,
live more, and design your best life!"*

My wish for you is to unplug, slow down, let go, tune in, and open up to living your best life. I believe every person is meant to shine and share their light without burning out. When you unplug from the daily hustle, redesign your life, and live aligned with your truth and inner wisdom, it's truly effortless, magical, and rewarding. I've learned that your purpose has seasons and is not what you do but who you are! The more you know yourself, the easier it is to live in alignment, and your purpose will evolve as you do. I'm your biggest cheerleader, here to support your purposeful journey of creating a life that you love!

Letting Go of Being Superwoman

It's Christmas Day—a day of joy, hope, peace, and love. A day to spend with family, share gifts, and exchange laughter. Not for me, though. Not today. I find myself driving in a daze, with my husband in the back seat, on my way to the emergency ward of the closest hospital. My husband has just tried to kill himself.

As I look in the rearview mirror, seeing him slumped to the side, I can't help but question who he has become. He was once my everything, but now

I struggle to recognize the person I married. I wonder if I still love him. After the past few years of trying to navigate his diagnosis of bipolar disorder, supporting his journey toward better health, getting him on the right medication, and attempting to make him happy while enduring his episodes of mania, depression, and emotional abuse, it's difficult to answer that question.

At this moment, love feels irrelevant. What matters is getting him to the hospital and ensuring his survival. Dread, disbelief, and hopelessness flood my emotions, leaving me feeling trapped. But in trying to fill the role of superhero, I put on my cape and just keep driving. I can't afford to think about myself right now. My focus is solely on getting him the help he needs.

I am in a terrible situation, yes, however, our lives didn't just all of a sudden fall apart on this Christmas Day. Over the last 2 dreadful years, I had been making choices that led me to lose myself and give everything to a toxic relationship. I sacrificed my own health, enduring emotional breakdowns and handing over financial control to someone who couldn't manage it, almost driving myself and my family into bankruptcy. I accepted constant emotional abuse and anger, allowing it to erode my happiness and mental well-being. I had poured so much of myself into my unhealthy marriage, attempting to fix, save, and heal my unhappy husband, that I experienced an emotional breakdown and severe burnout. There was nothing left of me. I was drained of all life force and vitality. Due to those choices, I was watching the story of my life, and letting someone else be the star in it.

Christmas was the final straw. Something needed to change. Finally, I tapped into my courage, decided to love myself more, and chose to be my own hero. In the new year, I found my voice, and I whispered, "I want a divorce." At that moment, I made a different choice, a life-changing one. I knew he would likely hurt himself again, and he did for a second time. It was his way of getting my attention and keeping me trapped in a marriage he was too fearful to let go of, even if it was no longer working for either of us. Although I cared for him deeply, it was not my responsibility to fix or save him. Each of us needed to take charge of our own personal health and well-being; I knew I had to leave to save my soul.

I ensured he was looked after and on his own 2 feet before walking away on mine. 3 months later, I had signed the divorce papers and found myself on a plane embarking on a new exploration. I made decisions that supported me and my happiness. I went on an adventure, my own personal 'Eat, Pray, Love' journey. Over 9 months, I traveled to India, Bali, and Australia. I engaged in activities that brought me joy, freedom, and balance, such as living in an

Ashram, visiting warm places with beaches, sunshine, and happiness, and doing 4,644 Yoga Sun Salutations for charity. This was my healing yoga quest, my Follow the Sun journey.

During this time, I allowed myself to think, dream, and rediscover who I was. I found myself at The Yoga Barn Wellness Centre in Ubud, attending a creative manifestation workshop. The facilitator, a tanned hippie soul, leaned over and asked, "Sharni, what do you want to manifest in your life?"

I listened to my inner voice and responded, "I want to create *this* same healing journey for other women." In that moment, something within me sparked, and I felt a resounding "YES" throughout my being; a full-body affirmation that tingled with excitement. I wished to support other ladies who had also lost themselves. It was a big first step towards fully living my best life. This led to creating a business I loved that inspired women to follow their purpose and have the courage to heal themselves.

In the 7 years following my divorce, emotional breakdown, and healing journey, I dedicated myself to building my wellness company and proving that I could thrive independently. I poured my heart and soul into my work, establishing *Follow the Sun*, a successful yoga and women's wellness company. We had over forty people working across 2 cities in South Africa, facilitating corporate wellness programs. I ran my own yoga studio in Cape Town and organized international retreats worldwide. I had built a thriving business that positively impacted many lives. Then, as well as *Follow the Sun*, I opened another company, *Cape Town Yoga Experiences*, where we had exclusive rights to facilitate yoga mornings before an awe-striking sunrise on top of Table Mountain, one of Cape Town's most famous and picturesque destinations.

I loved what I did. I was making a difference and totally living my purpose. However, if I was truly honest with myself, I was doing too much. To the outside world, I seemed happy and free; yet inside, my body was in knots of anxiety, overwhelmed, and suffering from sleepless nights.

After one of my successful Women's Wellness Retreats, I found myself in paradise, on my favorite tropical island, Gili Air. There is no motorized transport on the island; you either walk, take a bicycle, or ride in a horse cart. This island is tiny. Walking around the whole island takes about an hour. It's the perfect place to unwind, de-stress and slow down. I found myself relaxing on a daybed with the gentle sun kissing my skin, white beach sand between my toes, salt in my hair, a frangipani flower behind my ear, and sipping on a yummy fresh young coconut. Reflecting on the day, I thought to myself that I *should* be loving Life. I was not!

That is the thing about trying to be Superwoman. On the outside, it may seem we have it all together and live the perfect life, but we often feel trapped, depleted, and exhausted. I didn't even realize these familiar feelings had returned because I was too busy, too rushed to listen to my body's messages. Trying to be a hero for others had taken its toll on me. I had been pushing myself too hard for far too long. My body was shutting down, just like it had during my previous burnout episode. I recognized the symptoms of *Superwoman Syndrome*: chronic fatigue, headaches, nausea, dizziness, and fainting spells. This time, however, it was not just emotional exhaustion from my divorce but also physical and mental burnout from my work and running multiple wellness businesses. I had given so much of myself that there was nothing left to give.

When I finally took some time out to listen to my inner wisdom and have this moment of clarity on the beach in paradise, I realized she was saying, *You need space, dear Sharni.* She whispered, *You need to stop. You need to say no. You need to let go. You need to stop giving to everyone else and remember to look after yourself.*

The highly-driven version of me thought that I could condense my recovery into a matter of weeks. I was wrong. The cost of trying to be Superwoman and living with constant stress was immense. Even though I was living my purpose and loved what I did, I had to sell my beloved business, *Follow the Sun*. I had nothing left to give and lacked the energy to continue running it and supporting my clients. Medical bills drained my savings, and I had no income for about 2 years. I isolated myself from the world, cutting off social media and disconnecting from friends and family. The most devastating cost was the impact on my health, which was severely debilitating.

Burnout manifested in various health issues. I couldn't get out of bed in the morning as I felt too fatigued, faint, and sad. I cried all of the time and my brain was in a cloud of fog. My body was in so much physical pain, aching constantly, and I was so stressed that I even stopped menstruating. My body remained in a constant state of fight or flight, and even extensive rest and time in a Bali Ashram provided no relief. My emotional well-being suffered, leading to feelings of failure, low self-worth, and a lack of confidence. For a normally positive person, I had a very negative mindset. I was irritable, angry, and stuck in constant fear and lack mode. I dropped balls, I let people down. I didn't have the energy to face the world, and I didn't like the person I had become.

Eventually, after hitting rock bottom, I had no choice but to let go and redesign my life. It wasn't just about self-care practices like yoga and healing activities or indulging in bubble baths and massages. I was already doing all that! I needed to delve deeper into my life choices, unhealthy patterns, and limiting beliefs that held me back. Over eighteen months, I let go of everything that no longer served me. I redefined what success meant for me, realigned my work-life balance, redesigned and simplified my daily routine, and officially relocated to Bali. The most significant shift came from realizing that not only was I trying to be Superwoman, but I was also a people-pleasing, perfectionist 'YES' girl, who aimed to save the world and everyone in it... all on her own.

This realization helped me break free from the superhero mindset. I slowed down, simplified my life, reconnected with my inner wisdom, and tuned in to my more feminine energy of being gentle on myself and having more compassion toward myself. Instead of pursuing being perfect, I embraced being real. There was no point in striving for a successful business if it was not scalable and sustainable as well. I admitted I was the 'burnt-out yogi,' acknowledged that I needed help, and embarked on my own recovery program. Through this journey, I transformed my life from burnout to bliss and from feeling trapped to being free!

It took time and effort, and eventually, my life was entirely transformed. Happily, I fully recovered from burnout and became my balanced, gentle, feminine, magnetic *Shiny Queen*-self instead. I stayed in Bali, completely location independent, connected to a conscious community that nurtures my soul, and worked a few hours a day online, at a chilled co-working space or facilitating at The Yoga Barn. I spent my time going to healing sessions, doing my yoga practice, connecting with friends, laughing, singing, dancing, traveling, and living a simple life with less stuff and less stress. My favorite island, just off Bali, still served as my refuge, a place where I found peace and connection with nature and myself. During my extended stay on the island, I embarked on a 100 hour Yin Yoga Teachers Training, which empowered me to let go of the stressed and anxious Sharni I once was. I felt clear, calm, and deeply connected to Mother Earth, to the Universe, and most importantly, to myself. The combination of Yin Yoga, breathing, meditation, nature, and giving myself space and time for self-reflection has worked wonders in my life and guided me back to my purpose.

The ocean is my healing space. At sunrise, before morning yoga, I love to grab my Stand-Up Paddleboard (SUP) and head to the water. I often take the women on my retreats out for a SUP yoga session, but one particular morning I found myself alone. I spent 2 hours floating on my board, basking in the warm turquoise waters and gazing at the turtles swimming beneath me. It was breathtaking. My body soaked up the gentle sparkling sunshine, I could smell the fresh, clean air as I gazed at the bright, colorful, peaceful island before me.

That is my happy place. It's an experience that nurtures my soul and allows me to have meaningful conversations with myself and the Universe.

In those moments of serenity, I pondered my purpose in life. I had released my previous businesses. I had healed from my health challenges. I had learned so much more about myself and how I function. And, after transitioning from my marriage and not having had the opportunity to become a mother, I found myself questioning, *what to do next?* As I closed my eyes, allowing myself to be held and rocked by the gentle ocean, and just *be* in that moment… I asked the Universe, *What is my purpose now?*

Time seemed to stand still. I gently opened my eyes, and spotted a white feather in front of me, floating on the water. Feathers have a significant meaning for me and often appear in the most unusual of places. They show me I am on the right path and instantly I know it's a message from the Universe and my Angels, a sign of guidance. At that moment, a profound download of inspiration and insight descended *into* me. It was magical, powerful, and I knew this was the next step of my journey to living on purpose. All the puzzle pieces of my life fell into place.

I realized that my decades of studying wellness, and ancient healing techniques, and my twenty-year-long personal development journey combined into a powerful roadmap for others to redesign their life and find joy, freedom, balance, and healing in their lives. I needed to go through it all *myself* so that I could fully embody and experience how to shift and transform. Now, I have the full download, I have the *Magic Method* and I am ready to share my wisdom with the world.

I could have stayed married and kept myself in that toxic relationship, blaming the world for my unfortunate circumstances. I could have stayed in that Superwoman mode of trying to fix and save everybody and losing myself completely in my work. But I didn't, because to be honest my body wouldn't let me. In continuing to listen to my inner voice and intuition, finding balance and connecting more to my Yin feminine energy, and being gentle on myself, I finally found my true path forward. I learned I can manifest all that I desire… but by doing a little bit less!

You can stress less, live more, do less, be more, strive less, and thrive more! Bring more Yin to your Yang so you can slow down, let go, tune in, and wake up, radically redesigning your life by *Living Yinly.* By taking the pressure off of trying to be Superwoman and just learning to be more YOU—your messy, fabulous, feminine self—you will become your own hero, and design your very best life.

IGNITE ACTION STEPS

Here are The 5 Steps to Redesign Your Life by *'Living Yinly.'*

Step #1 – LET GO: Release what no longer serves you and rewrite your story. Declutter, clean out, and let go of anything holding you back. What is the next step you can take to clear the path toward living your best life?

Step #2 – RECHARGE: Prioritize self-care and nourish your body, mind, and soul. Engage in wholesome activities like exercise, yoga, and mindfulness to strengthen the mind-body-soul connection. Create space so you can connect to your inner wisdom and intuition. What is the next step you can take to slow down and tune in?

Step #3 – ENVISION: Discover your life's purpose and pursue your passions. Embrace your unique gifts and explore how they can make a positive impact. What is the next step you can take to start planting the seeds, living on purpose, and envisioning your ideal life?

Step #4 – FLOURISH: Cultivate fulfilling relationships and nurture self-worth. Find your tribe, open to the power of love, and allow your life and relationships to bloom. What is the next step you can take toward a flourishing life and thriving relationships?

Step #5 – MANIFEST: Unlock abundance in all areas of life. Improve your money mindset and embrace the art of manifesting. What are your next steps to invite abundance into your life as well as paying it forward?

Sharni Quinn — Cape Town, South Africa, and Bali
Certified Life Transformation Coach, Wellness Consultant, International
Yoga Teacher, Speaker, Author
www.sharniquinn.com
sharniquinn_wellness
sharniquinn_wellness
Sharni Quinn

Purpose Prompt 4

PRACTICE DAILY AFFIRMATIONS

Words have power. They can determine who you are, what you do, and where you go when it comes to serving your purpose. Who do you want to be? What do you want to achieve? Say it out loud.

Examples: I am filled with infinite possibilities for my Purpose. I am capable, worthy, and ready to fulfill my purpose. I am stepping into purpose of.... right now

I am

_____

I am

_____

I am

_____

I am

_____

I am

_____

I am

_____

Purpose Prompt 5

TAKING ACTION WITH PURPOSE

What small steps can you take daily to live a life more aligned with your purpose?

1. _____

   _____

   _____

2. _____

   _____

   _____

3. _____

   _____

   _____

4. _____

   _____

   _____

5. _____

   _____

   _____

Kathy A. Stubbs

Kathy A. Stubbs

"Your purpose on earth is to give your soul experiences."

Within our DNA, we have threads to all our generational and past lives that predispose us to our own belief systems. Family relationships… encounters with friends… teachers… all bring with them their own beliefs, patterns, programming, and imprints that interact and influence who you are. I want you to know, however, that you can release beliefs that no longer serve you through the process of forgiveness. My story shows the complexity of those relationships, the need to survive, and how your purpose can change throughout your life.

Massaging the Truth

I grew up in the Baby Boomer generation, born to a family I chose before this lifetime. Media and Dr. Spock's book influenced my mother on how to raise children. My father was the wage earner, and my mother was the stay-at-home parent responsible for raising my sister and me while managing the household. At an early age, I strove to receive attention and love from my parents. I was needy and wanted my family to acknowledge and love me. I felt guilty and responsible for my parents' arguments and unhappiness. And I felt powerless to protect my little sister. The source of her pain was a family secret. As a child, I never knew why she was screaming, but the sound filled me with terror and fear. I wanted it to stop.

All that fear was affecting me physically, emotionally, and mentally. The metaphysical toll those traumas took manifested as physical ailments—eye issues (I did not want to see what was going on), asthma (stress, fear, and an aversion to my father's smoking), allergies (hostile feelings), emotional and mental reactions (angry, fearful, anxiety, shame, and lack of trust). My body was expressing what my mind was suppressing.

I learned early to be a fearful child, 'a scaredy cat.' My father wanted a son, and I tried to be a tomboy to gain his love and acceptance. It was to no avail. I felt invisible in his eyes unless I was in trouble. My mother warned me often of the punishment I'd face if I did something that might upset him. Once, as a child, I even attempted to kill myself by eating chalk because I feared the consequences of breaking my father's measuring tape. At such a young age, I pondered drastic measures.

I was not what my parents signed up to experience. There was no on-and-off switch to silence me to provide them with peace. Having a family was not the joy-filled time my parents were led to believe it would be. They, too, came from dysfunctional families. Abuse was common. Neither of my parents knew how to deal with their own emotions, let alone teach and listen to me. I later discovered they had self-esteem issues and childhood traumas that still lingered with them in adulthood. Transactional love was what they knew. My parents claimed their responsibilities to me were to provide a roof over my head, food to eat, clothes on my back, and transportation. Anything additional was a bonus in their eyes. Though I didn't consciously know it, the message was a gift. I took on this survival statement as a slogan for myself.

I was the black sheep of my family. I was inquisitive, a literal chatty Kathy, and had different beliefs. They could not trust me. In addition, my self-talk controlled my behavior and how I was reacting. I was empathetic; I took on other people's emotions and felt my own strong, irrational feelings. I blamed others for moments I didn't fit in, didn't feel loved, didn't feel worthy, blah, blah, blah. I was causing myself to get sick because I was stuffing my emotions. Still, I thought I had a connection to Spirit early on, and I often asked for help from within. I did not know exactly who I was talking to, but it felt comforting.

When I turned eighteen, it was a stressful, scary time for me. My parents were relieved I was leaving home and no longer their responsibility. All year I had looked forward to graduating. Then as it drew near, I started to feel depression and dread. There was no one I knew or trusted that could help soothe me or teach me how to maneuver the transition from being a kid to an adult overnight. My insecurities and criticism triggers were not helping me.

My choices seemed limited, and I had been told all my life not to expect much for or from myself. The belittling job considerations that I was coming up with seemed within easy reach but were just meant to get me by until I could get married and have a husband take care of me. I knew deep, DEEP down, I had more potential. Yet, this ingrained belief system rooted in generational trauma—the thought of not being smart enough—I could not shake off. My primary purpose at this time was to prove my parents wrong and succeed in this life. I was willing and motivated to bring meaning into my life, even if it began as an act of defiance.

I enrolled in a private non-degree business school and worked for room and board at my parent's insistence. I hated this idea, but I did not see any other recourse. Paying for schooling was going to be my first real financial debt. There was no going back home. This was a placeholder in my life. I felt lost, and my mind chatter did not help. I was worried about my future.

Then the shape of my life changed a bit. I met the man who would become my husband while he was on military home leave. When he left, we maintained a long-distance relationship for over a year. I chose to delay marriage until I completed business school, was working, and got the experience of living independently. Living alone was hard, exciting, and challenging with 3 other wild nineteen-year-old girls. After work one day, I came home and found my roommate had invited her boyfriend to move into the room I was sharing with her. Another time, my roommates' boyfriends stole a flashing street barricade and put it on our back porch. We moved it inside our apartment until we could move it elsewhere. I was so stressed that the police would discover the stolen barricade, and I would go to jail. Another roommate was peddling marijuana out of our apartment. What a memorable experience, and it was uncomfortable feeling powerless, not knowing what would happen next. Looking back, I knew I was being divinely protected.

My future husband and I came from similar family dynamics, from parents who did not leave each other when the going got rough, even if perhaps they should have. We brought the generational lessons and beliefs we'd grown up with into our relationship with each other. He was already accustomed to doing chores around the house, having patience, and he was my best friend. I love my husband, and he is a good man. We balance each other.

After we got married, we soon moved to a Naval base in Australia. The Navy housing helped ease our marriage transition and our need to support ourselves and be independent of our families. I was able to get a government job on the base. Living on the other side of the world, there was no running home to our families. There was little communication with our families for multiple years.

Even the letters I sent home were a challenge because my mind was faster than my hand, and I was not an exceptionally good proofreader.

We knew the importance of education, and after my husband's discharge, we moved to Colorado, and he went back to university. I worked to support him so he could get his master's degree. Even though I could have enrolled in university, I played the victim again because I maintained the belief that I was not smart enough. After my husband graduated, we found jobs, but his career remained the priority. I was in my late twenties, and starting a family was paramount in my life. The process of becoming a mother was challenging for me. I endured 3 miscarriages but did not share this experience with my family. I felt guilty enough. My husband did not express any emotion or support. I grieved in silence on my own. Later, I succeeded in birthing a beautiful, healthy baby boy and, 2 years after, a beautiful baby girl. I was grateful and satisfied with the size of our family and was ready to find satisfaction in my professional growth as well.

There I was, having big expectations after being told not to. I was intent on being a mother and advancing in my career. My husband and I were transitioning from survival mode to a materialist lifestyle as a 2-income family. The challenge was to balance our relationship, careers, children, and our own personal needs. Both of us were becoming stressed and overwhelmed, and we lost the ability to communicate and understand each other's desires. Neither one of us focused on how to improve our home life because our lives were already full. I was cranky and needed help with shared responsibilities and the children, and my husband was self-absorbed in his own life and career. He was in a new job, and he needed to make a good impression. He loved what he was doing, and all he knew from his upbringing was the pattern of being a provider while the wife took care of the kids. But my purpose in life was evolving and changing as well. As a new mother, I needed guidance. My friends were a *generous* resource. I tried to use my intuition to weed out the guidance I was receiving, whether it was good or not, and succeeded most of the time. I needed to provide stability for my children and me. When I got stressed out, I participated in occasional "pity parties" and discovered it was not beneficial to me or my family.

I cared too much about my connection to my parents, extended family, friends, co-workers… and I wanted to help or fix their situations. They were not always receptive to what I had to offer. My focus was on others rather than taking care of myself. I would be a SUPER mom and SUPER human in my job. My goal was to give my children the best possible life and opportunities. I wanted them to see all the love I was giving and the effort I was making. Their recognition was important to me. That made me ask myself. *Was I repeating my childhood patterns of the transactional love my parents had shown?* I recognized how my own physical, mental, and emotional stresses were affecting my children. I did not know anything about self-care. I was the last in line to receive any attention. As I became aware of my sensitivities, my stress increased and threatened to boil over. I needed a way out.

I read an announcement for an upward mobility job in my organization. It was an opportunity that would allow me to leave the clerical field for a male-oriented, white-collar job. I felt a spiritual push and became excited about pursuing that job. I was qualified, and it was an opportunity to be a more significant financial contributor. Entering such a transition in my life brought fear and echoes of my past negative self-talk, but I knew I had the courage and was willing to take a leap of faith regardless. I was willing to take the new job even though it would uproot my family and move us to a different town, testing both me and my marriage.

My husband and my biological family said they would not support me thoroughly, and I was devastated. But I *knew* that was my moment to embrace my purpose. I took the job and discovered my potential. My husband joined me a few months later. This new job changed my life. It was transformative. I could no longer claim I was not smart enough. My work responsibilities matched others with college degrees, and I attained my level of expertise through professional experience. I was manifesting career growth, self-confidence, and I was proud of myself.

Years later, same job, same family, new venue, we moved to Alaska. My career took me to remote areas of Alaska without roads. Access to these areas is by helicopter, floatplane, or boat, with the possibility of bear or moose encounters. Since I chose to do this work, I could not let fear control me. I understood the risk involved, and I accepted it. One of my field trips was to a remote island known for bear hunting. My assignment was to post a sign using precise coordinates on the beach. The closest place the floatplane pilot could park was a quarter mile from the location. I had to find the exact coordinates because the pilot had to stay on the plane. Walking the distance to where I needed to post the sign, I sang the only song that came into my head, "The Mickey Mouse Club," song... possibly to a group of watching bears. Again, I was certain my spirit was protecting me.

I was about to need Spirit's protection in a much bigger way. When I turned fifty, it was a monumental time in my life. The family secret I had never known came to a head and was exposed. My sister had been physically abused. I was livid when I heard the truth. The thoughts and memories streamed in, the sound of her screaming and the confused fear I had felt. Guilt broke my heart as I realized I couldn't protect her. I wrote a 'garbage letter' of 'word vomit' to my parents. This helped me to release the poison I felt amid the whole situation. In time I forgave them and myself and used all that I had learned to help me process the news. I also leaned on my purpose of healing and helping others to release and let go of myself from the past.

Through this time of healing, I continued to ask the Universe for help. There had to be more to my life and what impact I could make. Within a week, I started receiving messages about massage therapy: in newspaper headlines, random conversations, and storefront signs. It gave me pause as I began questioning, *Is this real? Am I receiving the Universe's answer?* I was within 5 years of retirement, and life was already giving me a boot in the butt to make a change. As optimism flowed through my heart, I became convinced of what I needed to do. The guidance from Spirit was helping me align with my future *and* my purpose. I was being divinely led toward becoming a massage therapist. All I had to do was be willing to act upon this guidance.

What was interesting is that I took this leap of faith even though I had never experienced having a massage myself.

I found a massage school that would cooperate with me so I could still work full-time. The plan was to complete the massage program and take the national certification test prior to my retirement. The plan worked out perfectly. I was creating a soul-driven purpose. I was ready to stretch, change and become something else. I was prepared to surrender and be my *true* self.

During the lockdown, I made a choice to shift my healing business from in-person treatment sessions to providing energetic healing treatments on Zoom™. This allowed me to share my skills and talents with a broader international audience. In 2020, I started taking classes from Marilyn Harper and learned to connect and receive messages from Spirit. Through this training, I successfully discovered I had the ability to be a divine link receiving profound messages of love, encouragement, and guidance for my clients. I trust the love I am receiving is what I have been seeking all my life. Practicing the delivery of these channeled messages with my clients, I developed the confidence to share divine communication during Facebook Live™ group sessions weekly. This was fulfilling my continued commitment to the Universe to share spiritual energy with humanity, and I felt entirely on purpose.

I have learned that my purpose in life is to be in service to humanity and to give my soul experiences. Energetic healing and channeling are my passion and my path to do so. Doing this work is a labor of love and gives me great satisfaction, trust, and knowing Spirit supports me. I teach and assist my clients in being open to receiving and asking for help, to clear and let go of all that no longer serves them physically, mentally, and emotionally. In addition, I focus on generational and past life work healing and clearing personality traits, patterns, programs, and illnesses from their DNA, ancestral lineage, and Akashic records.

I understand all humans currently on this planet have their own journey and purpose. It is not for me to say what is right or wrong. I am here to help those requesting my help; to assist them on their own journey of discovery.

You can discover your purpose and feel your own inner light. You can connect with Spirit and feel guided along your path. Pause and receive, knowing Spirit is in you. Trust that Spirit will show you the way. When you question, or wonder, go deep, really deep, and listen to that inner voice that wants what is best for you. Move through any limitations and discover your own self-love and self-care. Recognize that the most important person in your life is you. When you make yourself the star your purpose is revealed.

IGNITE ACTION STEPS

- Recognize you are the most important person in your life.

- Learn to release and let go of negative thoughts and emotions regularly.

- Release from relationships that no longer serve you.

- Forgive others and forgive yourself.

- Give your soul experiences.

- Learn to meditate and journal.

- Answer these questions and begin your journey to discover your purpose.

- What do you love to do?

- What are your values, skills, and talents?

- *What is your passion?*

Kathy Stubbs — United States of America
Jeremeil Energetic and Spiritual Services, Sole Proprietor
Author, World Renown Healer, Channeler, Speaker
jeremeil.com
🛐 *The Hourglass Transmissions Group*

Nicole Shantel Freeman

NICOLE SHANTEL FREEMAN

"You are an Eagle; Soar Fearlessly."

My intention is for you to embrace and embody who you are and your authentic self. I want you to understand that there's no need to fear, feel ashamed, or harbor regrets about your journey, as every experience has molded you into the person you are today, guiding you toward your purpose. Embody your story with courage and conviction, for it holds the key to who you truly are. Enjoy the journey and embrace it all... the highs, the lows, and everything in between. You were born for this!

EMBRACE YOUR INNER CHAMPION... YOU GOT THIS!

I am sitting in the audience among many people, eagerly awaiting to address the crowd who came to hear me. I am wearing a bold red dress and stiletto high heels that scream I am ready to deliver a powerful speech that will motivate the thousands of individuals in the crowd. As the mistress of the ceremony completes my bio, I am called up to speak. I grace the stage, walking with my head high, shoulders squared back, and chest filled with pride. My eyes graze at the crowd as they are alert and ready to receive inspiring words from the dynamic Nicole Shantel Freeman.

In the distant past, this was once the version of me that I envisioned, a world-renowned speaker, a force to be reckoned with. Deep within me, I always innately knew that I was destined for greatness, to be a world changer. Yet, in reality, I lacked the qualities of boldness, courage, and confidence *to actually do it.* I became paralyzed by fear due to the fact that I had made unwise decisions that led me to believe that I was not qualified to deliver a compelling message to an audience. *I thought to myself, "Who would listen to me, and why would they want to hear what I have to say?"* I have always known how to encourage and motivate others, but I struggled to do that for myself. I found it difficult to encourage myself because my poor decision-making blinded me.

However, encouraging people has always come naturally to me; I do it unconsciously, without even realizing it. In my career, people constantly mentioned that I should be on radio, television, or performing on stage, encouraging and empowering them with my words of wisdom and infectious smile. Colleagues and friends often told me that my sharing was supportive and just what they needed to hear. People often refer to me as their personal cheerleader with a captivating smile. Hearing what others had to say about me made me feel like I was needed in the world. The mere fact that I was encouraging individuals was pleasurable and delightful, something I felt born to do. It came naturally, but I didn't feel that being a great 'encourager' was the ultimate purpose for my life. It was crazy how my self-doubt spoke so much louder than the positive feedback of others.

I couldn't see where I was making a difference because I only saw myself *as* my flaws. I found it difficult to move toward my purpose. Many heavy blows that life threw at me left me seeing myself as one giant failure.

I encountered numerous hardships in my life, such as unplanned, highly emotional pregnancies, financial struggles, and my dreadful divorce, just to name a few. It felt like I was in a boxing ring getting beaten down by these enormous hits from life. After each mighty blow, I would attempt to get up just to get knocked back down by yet another. Having failure after failure left me feeling like I could do nothing right, *so why pursue my purpose or the calling on my life?*

Though people constantly said, "Nicole, you are destined for greatness. You are brave, strong, and courageous. You are confident and compassionate. You are doing a great job." I disregarded those words because the negative voice in my head always spoke louder. The disempowering thoughts kept saying, "Nicole, you are stupid. You are a constant screw-up. You can't get anything right." These words would repeat in my mind and caused my limited belief system, imposter syndrome, and self-sabotaging actions.

Some years later, as a single, independent, Christian woman leading a women's Bible study group, when I found out that I was pregnant, I was in not only disbelief but denial. I couldn't fathom the fact that I disappointed God, my church, my family, and myself. I didn't want others to know that I, a Christian woman, had gone against the Bible and was pregnant. In a delusional panic, I even contacted my gynecologist's office and explained that, for some strange reason, my period hadn't come in a while. I proceeded to ask for medication to give my period a hand in showing up for me. I could hear the laughter in the nurse's voice as she asked me when would be a good time to come to take a pregnancy test. I *really* didn't want to believe that I was pregnant and thought, *"Nicole, how could you mess up so badly?"*

With tears in my eyes, I dropped to my knees in the praying position. I looked toward heaven, pleading with God to bring an end to my pregnancy. With every fiber of my being, I just wanted God to make it go away.

My pleading to God turned into a daily routine for me until one day, while having an in-depth conversation with a happily married woman, desperate to have a baby, I had a drastic change of heart. That heartbroken, discouraged woman captured my attention with her soul-shattering words. She and her husband had been trying to get pregnant for years, and as she told me her journey of miscarriage after miscarriage, my stomach was tied in knots. There I was blessed to carry a baby, yet I considered terminating. With tears rolling down my cheeks, at that moment, I decided that I would repent and enjoy the beautiful blessing growing inside of me. I was, in fact, *chosen* to carry my incredible baby girl.

Ironically, I always viewed single mothers as resilient, resourceful, strong, courageous, and independent. They are carrying the weight of 2 people, earning for a household, managing monthly bills on a single income, and caring for children's physical, mental, spiritual, and emotional well-being while potty training, guiding, and teaching all on their own. Though I was selflessly doing those same things alone with my daughter, I viewed myself as always making mistakes. The fact that I had a baby and wasn't married in the eyes of the church was difficult for me to push past. I continued living my life simply by going through the motions. I found a way to cope, but my direction and purpose felt so far from me.

God never gives you anything you can't handle, but if you don't learn the lesson, He will keep giving it to you. Thirteen years later, I am back in the same predicament again; pregnant and single, leading a women's Bible study group and on the prayer team at church. *"Nicole, seriously, what is wrong with you? Can you exemplify self-control? What will people say? How will others view me?"* were just a few questions crowding my mind. Experiencing deep disappointment, I found myself in the exact same situation, questioning my own choices. Honestly, I was appalled and disgusted with myself. So much so that I contemplated having an abortion.

One of the reasons that pulled me back from making such a hasty decision was my insightful teenage daughter, my first born. I vividly recall her ninth-grade school interview prior to entering high school. The witty interviewer asks my daughter, "Dead or alive, who would you consider your hero?"

Without hesitation, she confidently and sternly said, "My mom, because she gets things done by being a single mother and still manages to be there for me and others when needed."

I had recently shared the news of my pregnancy with my daughter, and her immediate question to me was, "How do you feel about having a baby and not being married?" I was taken back at first and felt maybe she didn't approve. Her response to the interviewer about me being her hero was surprising, and the sentiment moved me.

While driving home late that night, the windows were down, and the warm night breeze passed through my hair. I explained to my daughter that she didn't have to pick me as her hero just because I was present at the interview. She began to assert herself and explain to me that though she understood that conceiving a baby while single was the opposite of what the Bible states, she was still excited to choose me as her hero, someone she aspires to be like. As I clutched the steering wheel, I burst into tears. Despite my flaws, my daughter still saw me as a role model; in her eyes, my true character overshadowed any mistakes I made.

I realized at that moment that my greatest accomplishment and source of immense joy is being a mother. However, motherhood has come with its fair share of obstacles to overcome. I recall when my oldest daughter fell seriously ill as an infant; her wheezing was unbearable, which caused difficulty breathing. Her condition worsened to the point where hospitalization was the doctor's only option. That happened on more than 1 occasion, leading to countless sleepless nights as asthma took over her body. Though lonely, weary, and exhausted, I would pray all night through the morning on her behalf, pleading for God to grant her some relief. Seeing my baby in such anguish made my heart ache.

My purpose was becoming clearer, and now as a mother of 2, I needed to align with the gifts God had bestowed upon me and the direction of my life.

Yet, sickness struck again and tried to invade my new baby's body and cause worry and fear in me. Seeing my baby's limp and lethargic body crippled my soul as I dialed 911. She had been violently vomiting as I was trying to get home after dropping off my oldest daughter at school. I frantically pulled over on the busy, congested highway to find vomit everywhere, all over the baby, the back seat, the floor; there was so much of it. Attempting to hold back the tears, I called 911. A woman stopped to assist me and offer support and encouragement. She informed me that she would stay with us until the paramedics arrived. Once again, my self-doubt and inabilities showed up, but I dug deep to stay in alignment with purpose for both myself and my girls.

Though the hours are long, the days are tiresome, and things get extremely messy, the rewards of motherhood are excellent... priceless. Regardless of the sleepless nights and still managing to show up for work in the morning in good spirits, motherhood energizes me! It lights me up and gives me strength that I never knew existed. Going through those dark times with my children has molded me into the powerful, fearless, unstoppable woman I am today. Without a doubt... being a mother has always moved me toward my purpose.

While working on a deeply personal, vulnerable project, I prayed for God's divine guidance and wisdom as I embarked on that endeavor. Unbeknownst to me, I was about to undergo a deep interpersonal transformation. I journeyed into my past, digging deep into traumatic situations, prompting a profound self-realization. During that inward reflection, I was awakened to all the empowering qualities that I, Nicole Shantel Freeman, exhibit as a woman. With a newfound clarity, I began to perceive that those old false narratives had caused fear, hindering me from recognizing that I was *already* living out my purpose. It was then that my perception of myself shifted. I learned that I possessed those qualities that I had 'admired' they were in me, also. Yes, we all make mistakes, but that is shaping us into the people we need to be.

I now love to serve as a beacon of light, attracting people with my encouraging words, infectious smile, and supportive nature. I failed to realize that I don't have to do anything in and of my own strength but in God's strength. Jesus is the only one who walked the earth that was perfect and without flaw, *so why do I feel that I must be perfect?* I began to realize that God wants me to surrender to Him and pursue my God-given purpose.

Whenever negative thoughts attempt to surface, I consciously cast them down and replace them with positive affirmations and uplifting scripture from the Bible. Embracing the realization that I held within me all the qualities I admired in other single mothers, I ran toward my purpose. I wholeheartedly embraced my identity as the dynamic single mom I had always been. My purpose is to live a life submitted to God while supporting others to live the abundant life that Christ sacrificed for. I truly understand that the purpose is twofold: to enrich and serve yourself and others. By using positive and affirming words echoing loudly in my mind, I became intentional in ensuring that positive words would always speak louder than any limiting thoughts.

After experiencing a divine shift and embracing my authentic self, I focused on my business, *Elevating Eagles*, where I humbly and joyfully serve and support my clients as a Christian life coach and mentor. I've been honored to share my uplifting and inspiring words as a speaker at various events. Additionally, I've had the pleasure of organizing and hosting a number of my own events. I am currently living the visions I had years ago, even though my reality differs slightly from those initial dreams. All in all, I am fulfilling my dream and loving life on purpose!

I pray that you accept that your purpose, the unique gift you're destined to share with the world, may not come beautifully wrapped with a fancy bow. It's most likely that your purpose will come from the depths of pain and hardship because according to Romans 8:28, *We know that God causes everything to work together for the good of those who love Him and are called according to His purpose for them.* You will gain strength from your enduring determination and unwavering perseverance. Your purpose hides amid anguish, where your soul is grieved, and peace seems elusive. Embrace the challenges for you shall discover your true calling within the uncertainty. Enjoy the journey… it's igniting your purpose.

> *Without a doubt, God will transform your pain and*
> *problems into your meaningful purpose.*
> ~ Nicole Shantel Freeman

Ignite Action Steps

May these action steps serve as a guide to support you as you embark on your journey, igniting your purpose. You got this; I believe in you!

- **Seek God** - Read and meditate on the Word of God. A connection with God's guidance will move you toward your purpose.

- **Develop a grateful attitude** - Gratitude journaling will fill your heart with thankfulness which will take you further faster. Remember, the highs and lows are all working for you and moving you toward your purpose.

- **Embrace and embody your calling** - Write down the steps needed to get you to your purpose and be intentional in making the necessary changes to move you forward in your purposeful life.

- **Rely on your support system** - Remember, life will happen, and you may need some positive reinforcement. Surround yourself with others who are like-minded, or look for the support of a counselor or coach to help get you through the tough moments of life.

- **Practice self-love** - Be kind to yourself in the midst of mistakes. Give yourself grace. Trust that God never makes mistakes; therefore, what is happening is unfolding purposefully. Everything in life is working *for* you, so love yourself while you are going through it.

Nicole Shantel Freeman — United States of America
Christian Life Coach, Encouragement Speaker, Author
Nicole Shantel Freeman
nicoleshantelfreeman

Liora Karps

LIORA KARPS

*"Trust that your heart has the capacity to hold and
feel all your emotions at the same time."*

I hope to share with you that even when the worst thing you can possibly imagine happens, there can still be hope. Hope for happiness growth—a full, beautiful, and meaningful life despite unimaginable loss. No one gets through their journey untouched by grief. We must be open to the possibility that the most difficult moments in our lives can lead us to the greatest places, places where gratitude and joy can be found, and, more importantly, can be felt completely. I wish for you to know and trust that your heart has the capacity to feel many different emotions, all at the same time, even when those emotions seem to be completely opposite. You do not have to feel joy *or* sorrow, gratitude *or* grief. Instead, consider that you are able to hold all these feelings side by side, experiencing each one wholly. When you do this, you are able to move from surviving to embracing the act of truly feeling alive and living life on purpose!

LEARNING TO JUST BE

In my half-dreamy, half-awake state I feel my husband Shaun gently brush a kiss on my cheek as he leaves to take our children to school. *That's sweet,*

I think to myself. He doesn't usually do that, not wanting to wake me when I'm on a break from teaching and sleeping in.

My day unfolds as it usually does. A quick check-in with my therapist. *How does anyone do life without a therapist?* A brief mental debate over whether I should call Shaun to say hi. *I know he is busy with work.* He is short-staffed, but I call anyway, and we have a quick catch-up before he rushes off, getting back to his clients.

I have no idea that this will be the last time I will hear my husband's voice. The man who I have known since I was 15 years old. My partner and soul mate, who I have built a beautiful life with. I have no idea the wrecking ball that is about to come my way...

As my sister arrives for an unexpected visit, my phone rings. Shaun's friend asks me, "Li, has anyone called you about Shaun? He has been stung by a bee! You need to go to the hospital now!" As my brain is trying to process all that is coming my way, I keep thinking, *Shaun, what is it with you and bees?* This was not the first time I had been called by a friend to be told Shaun had been stung and had a severe allergic reaction to a bee sting. Upon completing a hike in the remote Cederberg mountains two years before, he took a celebratory swig from a beer bottle where a bee had been hiding inside. Unbelievably, a hiking buddy had thrown an Epipen into his bag at the last minute, which saved Shaun's life that day.

Leaving my two children with my sister, I race to the hospital, calling Shaun's family on the way. My heart is pounding, and I struggle to catch my breath. I run into the emergency room, not getting the words out fast enough: "Husband! Bee sting! Is he okay?"

I am quickly led to a quiet office where I am told that, yes, Shaun has been stung; he is not at the hospital yet, they are trying to stabilize him at the scene. *What does that even mean?* My mind tries to comprehend their words, I am hearing them, but they make no sense. *Stabilize him?* I don't understand. *How bad is it?*

They tell me that when he arrives, they will not work on him in the emergency room but take him straight up to the ICU. Moments later, I hear doors fling open, voices shouting, and as I look out the doorway of the cramped office, I feel the whoosh of the stretcher, only seeing Shaun's feet as they rush him into the elevator. Then there is silence...

At that moment, my eyes are *seeing*, but I do not understand. Things *look* serious, but I still don't know how unstable Shaun's condition is. As the moments simultaneously crawl and fly by, my mom brings my children to the hospital.

"Where is Dad?" my daughter nervously asks.

"I don't know." I answer quietly.

"Is he going to be okay?" my son questions as he holds my hand.

"I don't know." I repeat, still in disbelief at what has happened.

They cry, "Can we see him?"

I feel powerless to comfort my children, but on some level, I know it would be worse to tell them everything is going to be okay when I do not know if that is going to be true.

The ICU doors swing open, and a doctor walks out. I feel a sense of relief, he is a friend. As he begins to speak to me, I am distracted by his eyes. I keep thinking to myself, *They are so red and puffy. Why would he be crying?* I manage to focus my mind on the words he is saying. "Li, the next twenty minutes are critical. I need you to know that this may not be okay. Shaun may not be okay. They have resuscitated him twice, and we just have to wait and see." All I can think is to ask, "Do you think we need to start a prayer group?" He pauses, then answers, "You definitely should."

The ICU waiting room is soon filled with family and friends. Our community grapevine works well, and word has spread that there has been an accident. I am grateful for the company and the support. I am going to need it.

Over the next few weeks and months, many doctors and specialists attend to Shaun. Multiple tests and scans are done. Therapists work on him. We moved to a more specialized hospital. We transitioned from the ICU… to a general ward… to a rehab ward. All the while, Shaun's condition remained the same. He lies in a state of unresponsive consciousness, or, in more medical terms, a persistent vegetative state. Shaun's test results and scans indicated that his brain had been severely damaged due to the lack of oxygen as a result of being stung. Even if he does wake up, he would not be the Shaun that we knew. My emotions were a mess, and I longed for Shaun, as he was my safe space. Always there. My anchor. Without him, I was adrift and unsure. The hours run into days, weeks, and months. I lost track of time, and everything I once knew was gone.

From the moment of the accident, the support is instant. An abundance of food is brought to the hospital each day. I stop making lunch for my children, who are still having to attend school despite their dad's condition. Motivational posters, luminous hearts, and beautiful messages decorate the hospital waiting room that had become my safe haven. Other people's love is what holds me up on the days I do not have the energy to hold myself up. As the overflow of care pours in, I struggle with not only receiving but embracing it. I sit quietly in a corner I have been using as a hideaway when I need a moment of solitude. I consider telling people that I am managing, but in truth, I am barely surviving.

I struggle at times to accept all the help, yet I have a moment where I realize that everyone's world has been rocked by this random tragedy, and they, too, feel helpless. No one can change what has happened or take the pain away. No one can magically make Shaun recover. The only thing those around us can do to feel that they are there for us, fulfilling a purpose, is through practical tasks: make a meal, help with a lift to school, and buy some household supplies.

Through these compassionate gestures, I understand the power of community. I have a choice to make. Pull away, go inward, and try to cope as best I can on my own, or allow space for others to support me. *If supporting me brings them some comfort, who am I to take that away from them?* I tell myself, *People want to be there for each other. We just have to decide to open up and let them in.*

As I become more comfortable allowing others to step up and support me, it has awakened in me an awareness of the blessings around me. My heart is shattered, and I am completely grief-stricken, but I also feel thankful for those around me and abundant appreciation for so many things; the delicious steaming cup of chai tea latte left for me by a friend who knows I don't feel like talking to anyone, *but I do love to drink chai tea!* My children's arms holding on to me a little tighter and longer each time we embrace. There is gratitude for the many strangers who have done their best to help me navigate systems that do not understand circumstances like mine. The manager at the bank who helps me access Shaun's account so that I can continue running his business. The lady at the cellphone store who helps me with Shaun's phone, and the gentleman at the supermarket checkout who comes round to hug me even though it is too hard to explain to him the reason for my tears. These are but a few examples of the beautiful gifts that have come my way while the life I once knew lies in ruins around me.

I have become aware that my heart can hold all my emotions at the same time, even when what I feel in a single moment seems like a jumbled mess of contradictions. Our hearts are amazing like this. We don't have to choose to feel one thing at a time. We can feel it all! I like to think of my heart as Neapolitan ice cream. *Why should you choose just one flavor when you can have all three?* As vanilla, chocolate, and strawberry can all swirl together in one delicious mix, sadness, joy, and anger can swirl, too.

Yes, I felt anger. Just ask the doctor who would not allow the speech therapist to see Shaun those first few weeks or the nurse who could not tell me when Shaun was last fed. They will tell you about an anger that took even me by surprise. Yet, I found tender moments with my children, enjoying one another, and gratitude when a friend sent a beautiful flower arrangement.

I hold each emotion as important, even the ones no one wants to embrace. A friend asks me, "How angry are you with G-d, on a scale from one to ten?"

That is the first time I have been asked that question, but I realize with some surprise that this is also the first time I have even considered the possibility that anger towards G-d is something I could be feeling. I fall silent and try hard to consider my emotions. *Do I feel angry with G-d? I suppose I should... it's an obvious and expected response.*

Yet, I am certain that I do not. I consider what I have always held to be true. I do not believe in a punishing, vengeful, spiritual entity that decides what terrible fate befalls certain people each day. There are no contracts made when we come to this life that state if we behave in a certain way, do or don't do certain things, we will forever be protected from suffering, grief, and pain. I do not know what the purpose of Shaun's accident is, but I do know with every fiber of my being that it was not a punishment... it is as it should be.

I believe our souls choose their experiences and accept their journey. I do not know why—what we are here to learn—but I do know that we have the choice to grow and transform or to become bitter and resentful. Does this choice to step into each day with an open and grateful heart take away from the pain we experience? *Of course not!* Does that mean we are okay with what has happened to us? *No!* But it has happened. It is done. All we can choose is *how* we move through each experience.

That means I am acutely aware that my children are watching me and will follow my lead. If I choose the, "Why me, life is terrible, I'm so angry with G-d" path, then that's what they will learn. That would be a tragedy on top of a tragedy. I am determined that will not happen.

A lot of the time, I feel untethered, overwhelmed, and incompetent. These are all uncomfortable feelings, but they are not anger. Of course, I get angry, but I choose not to stay there in that destructive space. I think of anger as a 'top of the pile' emotion. When Shaun used to get dressed each morning, I would often look at him and teasingly ask him how he chose that particular outfit. "How did it make any sense to you to match that top with those pants?" His response was always the same. "It's easy! They were on the top of the pile!" I see anger as the feeling that sits on the top of the pile of all my emotions. When I feel something uncomfortable and painful, it is so easy to just grab from the top of the pile. ANGER! But I have come to understand that anger does not leave much space for anything else. It fills us completely. It is consuming, making it difficult to hold gratitude, love, or appreciation at the same time. I now look a little deeper down through my pile of feelings.

Everyone has their own way of walking through their journey with grief. I am sharing my perspective and the choices I have made. Consider the words you use to label your emotions and trust that your heart can hold all those feelings simultaneously, just like that tub of Neapolitan ice cream.

I am a true type A perfectionist personality. I like to have complete control over every aspect of my life. *Well, this certainly showed me!* One day life was going along as planned, and the next, it had all collapsed around me. I couldn't change or control what had happened or what the outcome would be. As the days passed and I struggled to sleep, my physical and emotional energy depleted, I could feel that I had to start choosing carefully where to pour my energy. If I spent my days asking, *Why has this happened to us?* I would not have enough energy to be there for my children. If I tried to do it all on my own, I would be too exhausted to make the important decisions before me. Instead, I chose to surrender, recognizing what I cannot control and mindfully identifying what I can: my thoughts, the words I use, and my actions. I chose to move Shaun to a more specialized hospital. I chose to get up each morning and make an effort with my hair and makeup. *I can't control what I'm feeling on the inside, at least the outside will look half-decent!* I chose to find just one thing about each day that made me feel grateful, even if just for a minute: a small flower in the cracks of the paving, that first sip of coffee in the morning. They are small flickers of light in a big dark room.

After spending six months in the hospital, Shaun moved to a frail care facility where he continued to receive the best possible care. There was never any change to his condition. He remained unresponsive for three years, though pouring unconditional love into being present for him remained my purpose throughout that time.

Shaun developed a complication in July 2022 and passed away on the 8th of August, and I have since walked the path toward a new purpose, of sharing what this journey has taught me. When I share my story, and even as I read the words I myself have typed on this page, there is a part of me that sits outside myself for just a moment and thinks, *Shame! That poor lady!* The thought a second later is, *Oh my gosh! They are talking about you!* While yes, my story is tragic, this is not what I want people to think of when they think of me. This is not what I want you to remember when you turn the last page of my chapter. My story has made me into the person I am today, but it does not define me. The choices I have made on this journey, my perspective, and my newfound ability to feel completely, are the threads with which I continue to weave the Me I am each day.

I continue to hold the pain of Shaun's loss right next to my belief that this is as it should be. My children and I live with gratitude and choose to feel joy at the same time as our heartache. I am immensely proud of the person I have become, the choices I have made, and the growth that has taken place within me. I hold this next to the place that can't quite believe that this is my life now, and would give anything to have Shaun back. Through this journey, I have become acutely aware of and present to all my feelings, even the uncomfortable ones. I trust in my heart's capacity to hold them all at once. I know each is valid and true, that one takes nothing away from the other, and that they all serve a purpose. I am able to identify the few things I can control and surrender to the vastness that I have no say or choice over. As I continue this journey through my beautiful life with all its peaks and valleys, I am learning to sit in each moment, take it all in, and to *feel*. This is what I call *being purposeful* and learning to *just be*.

IGNITE ACTION STEPS

1. Create space for others to support you. Say yes to offers of help, even when your instinct is to say no. Become aware of those in your community who need you to step up and be there for them.

2. Become aware of the language you use to describe your emotions. Don't just grab the one that's on top of the pile! You don't have to choose one feeling at a time. Trust that your heart has the capacity to hold all your feelings, even when they feel contradictory. Your feelings will not break you! Learn to be in them.

3. Consider where you pour your energy. You can't control everything. Whilst you may not like the choices you have, you have choices. Surrender to everything else.

4. Choose to be grateful, even if it's only for one small thing each day. Open your eyes to your blessings as you hold your pain. Be present in as many moments as you can. There is always something good if you seek it with intention.

Liora Karps — South Africa
Teacher, Business Owner, Motivational Speaker
www.liorakarps.com
🅕 *liora.gorkkarps*
🅞 *liorakarps*

Purpose Prompt 6

USE YOUR TALENTS TO BETTER THE WORLD

Purpose appears when you combine what you value with what you're good at. Consider your key talents. How can you support your purpose by using these talents every day?

My top 3 talents are:

1. _____

_____

_____

2. _____

_____

_____

3. _____

_____

_____

These talents support my purpose by:

_____

_____

_____

_____

Purpose Prompt 7

ASK YOURSELF, 'HOW CAN I SERVE?'

Part of living on purpose is helping others. Find ways that you can give, serve, offer, and supply others with what you have and what they need. Through helping those in need, you provide them with the opportunity to discover their purpose in return.

I can serve others by:

_____

_____

_____

_____

_____

_____

_____

_____

_____

_____

Nicole Mixdorf

Nicole Mixdorf

*"Wholeness is always available to us anytime
by loving and radically accepting ourselves,
regardless of what is happening in our lives."*

May you be inspired to never be limited by the challenges in your life. Always look for something to smile about... for what you focus on will grow. Reclaim your wholeness and your healing as your birthright. Even in the darkest of moments, the light is always there to guide you back to yourself.

Smiling into Wholeness

I held the heavy wooden frame of my grandpa's funeral photo and stared at the permanent frown lines etched on his face. This wasn't how I remembered him at all, and that realization inspired something within me. I decided right then and there that I would live the rest of my life with a smile on my face every day instead of a frown, intentionally choosing happiness as my way of being.

I have always had a positive outlook on life. I grew up in Los Angeles with a loving family that cared deeply for one another. With my grandparents living only a mile away, my big brother and I would get on our bikes and ride up the giant hill to their house, huffing and puffing, where we'd be greeted at the door with warm embraces and smiling faces. My grandpa, who we called Papa, would play with us all day until *we* were tired. He was a loving man with us, even if he could be a stern man with others (no doubt the cause of those frown lines). I carry the memory of his smile with me and share that sense of happiness and loving energy with everyone I connect with.

Ask anyone who has ever met me, and you'll quickly find out that I truly live my life smiling all day. Even on my darkest days, I find positive things to focus on. If I make eye contact with a stranger, I will immediately smile with my whole being and say hello. People can feel the uplifted energy I exude through my smile, which comes from the deepest part of my soul and emanates through my sparkling eyes. This is a big part of my identity, and how I connect with the world. I believe that each smile I share with someone has a beautiful ripple effect, elevating their energy and resulting in them smiling back. Perhaps they'll smile at the next person, and that person will smile at someone else. Smiles are contagious in the most beautiful way.

Throughout my life, I have always wanted to inspire everyone around me through my words, attitude, mindset, and actions. Inspiration is interwoven into the light codes of who I am. Even when I was in high school, I often used my ability to give powerful advice to my friends about the best way to navigate through their challenges. I could effortlessly pull them out of despair and elevate them to a place of empowerment to see the situation from a higher perspective. It was natural for me to lift people up and inspire them to believe in themselves, and I prided myself in having the perfect words to say. It would be another decade before I did this professionally, but reflecting on my life, I can see that inspiration was always in me.

Yet, a decade after graduating, I would face a reality that shook the core of who I am. Life took a painful turn when my sweet daddy was diagnosed with cancer, and it felt like a rug was pulled out from under me. As I had done in my life, my dad put up a smiling face whenever he was around others, exuding positivity and confidence that he would push through. All the stress from my father's illness, combined with the stress from my corporate job, started making me sick. I developed a debilitating condition called ulcerative colitis that causes bleeding intestinal ulcers and an immediate sense of urgency to use the bathroom. One moment I would feel fine, and the next, my stomach would cramp with stabbing pain, forcing me to run to the bathroom hoping I would get there in time. This agonizing situation would happen up to twenty times per day.

I couldn't function that way and I knew that I needed help to heal and feel whole again, which led me to a wellness retreat with Deepak Chopra. A beautiful and profound question found its way to me that changed the trajectory of my life. *What is my purpose?* As I reflected on this question, more arose: *What are my passions and special gifts, and how could I use them to serve humanity? What am I here to do? Why did I choose this life?* I formed a daily practice of asking myself those questions with a yearning for the answers and then releasing them to the Universe with complete surrender. The answers were all within me. Once I calmed my mind and brought more peace into my life, they started flowing into my consciousness.

I dove into self-care, committing to a daily practice of yoga, breathwork, and meditation. My yoga mat was my sanctuary, and every time I unrolled it, I felt the stress start to fall away as I grounded myself within. I also focused more energy on incorporating joyful activities into my daily life, like painting and gardening, which brought my personal wholeness back into alignment. Strengthening that part of me was key to maintaining my sanity and providing my body with the rest and rejuvenation needed to function and heal.

Amazingly, the symptoms I had been experiencing started to resolve once I released stress and prioritized self-care. It was at that point that I received an epiphany that my purpose is to INSPIRE! I wanted to inspire other executives and busy professionals to find balance in their lives so they could heal and thrive, also. This is what led me to start my award-winning corporate culture and well-being company, Balance by Nature®.

Tapping into this purpose brought incredible meaning to my life. There was something so powerful about knowing exactly who I was, what I wanted, and what I was meant to do. It felt like a magnet was pulling me forward toward my calling. I started stepping out on stage as a keynote speaker, inspiring audiences to believe in themselves; to know that they were whole and here to fulfill a mighty purpose, also.

I wish I could tell you it was all peaches and roses from there, but that's not how this story goes. Each time my dad had a recurrence of cancer, my debilitating flare-ups of bleeding ulcers would follow. I calmed the fiery symptoms down using Western medicine and changes to my diet, which only gave me temporary relief. This condition reared its ugly head every time I experienced intense stress, which would leave me depleted and exhausted, stuck in the bathroom all day in pain.

Then, I experienced my first miscarriage, which happened to be a twin pregnancy. It was an emotional rollercoaster to go from weeks of excitement and love to sudden loss and utter devastation. Fortunately, I was blessed to get pregnant again right away, which was a beautiful miracle that I was endlessly grateful for. Life took an unexpected turn when complications arose at the end of my pregnancy, resulting in an emergency C-section to save my baby's life. My 3-pound baby spent his first 3 weeks in the NICU at the hospital, and it was at that time that we found out my daddy only had 3 months left to live. I remember the feeling of my son's warm tiny body pressed against my chest as I cried in that hospital room, with the sounds of a million monitors beeping simultaneously in the background, drowning out my cries. I envisioned my baby's future, and from the deepest parts of my heart, wished him a sense of wholeness that I instinctively knew was his birthright.

3 days later, I found out that a substantial corporate deal I had been working on for my business for a year and a half had just fallen apart at the last moment. *What was happening?* These heavy circumstances led to another flare-up of colitis while I was still healing from my C-section. My physical, mental, and emotional wholeness had already been deeply affected, and now this hurricane was impacting my financial, social, and professional wholeness as well!

Birthing new life into the world as it was being taken from my dad was a deeply painful and spiritual experience. My dad lived to meet his first grandchild. I saw the entire cycle of life in its fullness. Having a beautiful baby to care for took some of the pain away from losing my daddy, but losing him also took some of the sparkle away from having a new baby.

Being a preemie, my son had additional needs, requiring weekly appointments with the pediatrician, lactation nurses, physical therapists, and other specialists. Needless to say, I was overwhelmed by everything I was dealing with. I decided to take 8 months away from my business so I wouldn't drown from my lack of mental wholeness. I navigated my way through illness, loss, grief, motherhood, and the whopping eighty-six appointments I had to take my son to during his first year of life. This stress preceded even more emotional pain as I entered a deeply tragic period of loss and grief in my life when I also lost my other grandpa, my cousin, my grandma, and 2 more pregnancies in short order. And, of course, physical pain came with it. Bleeding ulcers flared up after each loss, intensifying the challenge I was going through. I'm not sure which was worse, the mental and emotional pain of loss or the physical pain from the illness that inevitably followed.

Somehow, the truth of who I am at my core would keep resonating as I pulled myself out of these painful moments. Over time, as my baby's needs began to calm down and I had the space to dive back into my work, I was driven forward again. I used my business and purpose to anchor me during those difficult times, which lit me up inside in the most profound way and allowed me to regain a semblance of balance so I could keep smiling as I inspired others to heal. I wouldn't let anything stop me from pursuing my big dreams. Even in the darkest of moments, the light was always there to guide me back to myself.

A couple of years later, I was blessed with a deeply spiritual experience that allowed me to call my daughter's soul into my life. After having my third miscarriage, I started receiving signs of turtles from my daddy's spirit that gave me immense peace and comfort, knowing that he was with me and protecting me. I held as my truth that my dream of having another baby would become a reality, and I started seeing turtles everywhere! There was a turtle on my wall calendar that month. A plant a neighbor brought me had a small turtle figurine at the bottom. I opened Facebook to have a turtle picture greet me as the first thing in my feed. The towel my son left on the bathroom floor had a turtle on it. I didn't know what was happening, but I felt divinely supported, like something bigger than myself was occurring, and it gave me such a profound peace that lifted me above any pain of loss. Sure enough, my sweet and healthy rainbow baby came into our lives the following year, completing our family and once again reminding me of everyone's birthright for wholeness.

Then my miraculous high was coupled with another low. I had a terrible flare-up of colitis after my daughter was born, which did not respond to traditional Western medication. I got extremely ill, getting down to one hundred and five pounds, forcing me to stop nursing my baby because it was too depleting on my body; a devastating realization that something significant needed to change in my life. The doctors had no answers for me, so I embarked on a remarkable journey to heal my body naturally since I was connected to a vast network of wellness practitioners and healers. I wasn't going to let the doctors place their limitations on me. It was time to find *my* healing and wholeness.

Over the next eighteen months, I worked with fourteen different holistic healers on my quest to reverse the dis-ease that had been plaguing me for so long. It would have been really easy to give up and become a victim, but that's not me. I never stopped searching for my answers. After five hundred forty-seven days of bleeding every single day, I was introduced to a Chinese Divine Healing Master, who blessed me with an exquisite and unique energy healing miracle that gave me my life back. I was spontaneously healed, and I threw a party to celebrate!

Throughout all the challenges I experienced, I never let anything stop me from pursuing my dreams. Even when I was frail and weak, taking care of a newborn baby and a rambunctious 4-year-old boy, I still met with my clients and smiled every day. Happiness was a choice that I made on a daily basis, regardless of what was happening in my life! Remembering my Papa, I decided that I was going to live my life with a smile on my face each day. Something beautiful was always happening, and it was up to me to find it. The more I leaned into gratitude for what was going well in my life, the more my mental and emotional wholeness was strengthened.

During a deep meditation one night, a powerful visualization formed of me speaking on the largest stages in the world. I was holding up my hands to share healing light with the crowd as I inspired them to awaken to the truth of who they are and what they are capable of. A message came through so clearly: *my soul's divine contract was to raise the collective vibration on the planet, and I would do it in this life or the next*. I felt that powerful choice before me to decide if I would fulfill my soul's purpose now or later.

I knew this was a pivotal moment in my life. As I sat in the profound energy and activation of that blissful divine experience, I decided and declared to the Universe that I was choosing THIS LIFE to fulfill that divine purpose. I will change the world in THIS LIFE!! *My purpose is to inspire people to believe in themselves, to heal from within, and reclaim their wholeness and inner power to live their best expression of life.* This is my contribution to the divine plan, and it is my chosen destiny to fulfill it now.

My journey to healing and wholeness got me thinking about what wholeness really is. When life was falling apart around me, I didn't feel whole, and it pulled me out of balance, making me feel like a shell of myself. I leaned into self-care, holistic healing modalities, my spiritual practices, my tribe, and my mindset to bring me back to myself. Upon reflection, I have identified what I consider to be the 10 Pillars of Wholeness, which make up all the multifaceted aspects of our lives.

1. **Personal Wholeness:** Passions, interests, hobbies, travel, self-care, personal development, and education

2. **Mental Wholeness:** Mental state, self-talk, mindset, stress load, and resilience

3. **Physical Wholeness:** Health, diet, nutrition, fitness, and sleep

4. **Social Wholeness:** Romance, parenting, family, friends, colleagues, team, tribe, and social media

5. **Financial Wholeness:** Relationship with money, healing old money stories, manifesting abundance, financial literacy, estate planning, and retirement

6. **Energetic Wholeness:** Personal energy, vibration, motivation, drive, gratitude, and manifestation

7. **Professional Wholeness:** Career trajectory, brightness of future, goals, mindful leadership, productivity, and intentional time management

8. **Environmental Wholeness:** Home, office, neighborhood, community, planet,clearing clutter, organization, being of service, and sustainability

9. **Emotional Wholeness:** Emotional state, breaking through limitations, releasing anger and pain, transcending grief, forgiveness, and healing from trauma

10. **Spiritual Wholeness:** Connection within, intuition, purpose, vision, and faith

When any one pillar doesn't receive enough attention or has too much negative energy associated with it, life gets pulled out of its delicate balance, and we don't feel whole. When I held the intention of bringing my different pillars of wholeness back into alignment, it allowed me to experience balance, giving me the strength and a frame of mind to find my way out of the darkness and back into the light.

I am fulfilling my divine purpose by sharing my wholeness journey with others so they can bring their lives back into alignment, just as I have. I am at the forefront of a shift from corporate wellness and well-being into corporate *wholeness*. I am guiding global brands to integrate wholeness into the culture of their businesses to increase employee engagement, reduce attrition, and improve health outcomes.

My journey to reclaim wholeness guided me to heal from the inside out, through every layer of who I was, so I could step into the truth of who I came here to be. Most importantly, I learned that wholeness is always available to us anytime, by loving and radically accepting ourselves regardless of what is happening in our lives.

If you are going through a significant challenge in your life right now, I encourage you to take a step back and evaluate which pillars of wholeness are being affected. When any of them are out of alignment, they start impacting other areas of our lives as well. It's important to intentionally focus on strengthening the other pillars so you can be supported as you navigate the challenge.

Perhaps you are dealing with a relationship falling apart, losing a job, financial worries, or caring for a sick parent. Regardless of the type of challenge, the stress may start impacting your mental and emotional pillars. If left unchecked, it could eventually turn into health issues, impacting your physical pillar as well. It's important to focus attention on strengthening those areas of your life, along with your personal, energetic, and spiritual wholeness (which are often the first to get neglected when life gets stressful) so that you can maintain a sense of balance as you find your way out of the darkness.

Life doesn't have to be perfect in order to feel whole. Bring balance back into your life by aligning your pillars, one at a time, as you navigate the intense storms and beautiful rainbows that follow. Always look for things to be grateful for, especially during the hard times, as it will remind you of how very blessed you really are. I hope that you can love and accept yourself at this moment to reclaim your wholeness as you step into your greatness with a big smile on your face.

IGNITE ACTION STEPS

- Looking through the 10 Pillars of Wholeness, write down which main pillars are out of alignment in your life. Then write down which additional pillars they may be affecting. Pick one pillar to start with. What is one small step you can take to strengthen it? Make a plan and get started.

- Write down how you can prioritize your personal wholeness more. What brings you joy? What lights you up inside? Schedule at least twenty minutes of these fun activities into your *daily* calendar.

- Create a daily practice of asking yourself *What is my purpose? How can I help? How can I serve?* The world needs more awakened souls fulfilling their destinies!

Nicole Mixdorf — United States of America
Speaker, Author, Founder & Chief Wholeness Officer Balance by Nature
www.balancebynature.com
nicole.nadelmixdorf
nicole.mixdorf
nicolemixdorf

Eric LG Longoria

Eric LG Longoria

"The brighter your light, the clearer your journey."

No matter where you come from, you have the potential to become limitless. I've had chapters in my life where I thought my purpose was fitting into the world's view of success. I hope by reading my story, you'll realize it's not the world's job to assign your purpose. Sit with yourself, reflect, and listen to what your heart is telling you and where it's guiding you. As you release your past, embrace the changes you feel. The light inside of you will shine so brightly revealing your path ahead. As you put in the work, you'll start seeing things that were distorted or dark more clearly. Your breakthrough is coming; follow your light!

Releasing Arrows

"Sh*t. I'm gonna die."

The buildings were in ruins, and smoke still lingered in the air. But *this* felt like I had reached the end. Our convoy was surrounded by thousands of protestors as we exited through downtown Baghdad. Angry citizens tried to climb onto my gun truck and overtake me. I sent prayers up to God in the surrender of my own death. This gave me the fight to carry on through the missions to come. I had listened to the countdown on the way there: "3 hours 'till Baghdad."

"2 hours 'till Baghdad." Our platoon had survived driving through an IED Alley, past camels, and miles of empty desert. We drove through a warzone in the area surrounding Najaf, which was devastating. I didn't see myself coming out of it. *Was I meant to be here?*

After graduating high school, I tried to figure out what I wanted to do with my life; what my purpose was. My father was a Marine, and I didn't see myself finishing college, so I decided that the military was the best option for me. At nineteen, I joined the Army, which brought me to Baghdad. I would do 3 tours in Iraq before I was through. The things I experienced, like the loss of my comrades, weighed on me heavily. The close calls I endured during my military career had changed me. I imagined myself retiring from the military after completing my twenty years, but that didn't go as planned. I ended up retiring early due to service-connected injuries, and my life changed dramatically.

During the 2008 global financial crash, I lost my house, my relationship, and I was getting retired from the military—all at the same time. I saw nothing ahead of me; the military was the only purpose I had known. It seemed like all life's doors had closed for me, so I went home to Arizona to plan my next steps. My fresh start felt like a real soup sandwich, but I decided to drive on, let it go, and move forward. I didn't reflect on anything. I just continued to push, grind, and hustle to make it to 'success.' But I didn't know exactly what that was. I realized I was just trying to "make things happen." This is what I was programmed to do.

I started a little business, but it wasn't profitable. I didn't understand the business dynamics and the industry at the time. I decided to go to college, thinking it would show me how to reach the upper ranks of the business world. I discovered there was a lot more to business than I first thought. I could apply the skills I had learned to get a good-paying job, but there was always something missing. I didn't feel like I belonged. I didn't like the whole 'dog and pony show' to get a paycheck. This couldn't be the game plan; there had to be more. *Where do I belong?*

I was a hard worker and did well at my job. I was always trying to bring the business to the next level. Yet, I receive a lot of pushback, "Slow down!" "You're not in the military anymore; chill." "Everyone thinks you're the manager." "Why are you trying to help me? Are you trying to take my job?" This made me feel alone, confused, and defeated. As time passed, I felt obsolete, like a washed-up veteran. I was able to go to war and survive, but I couldn't figure out how to fit in once I got back. I knew I didn't want to work in my current profession anymore, but the change in industries made my transition even more difficult. I felt lost. I was disconnected. I wondered, *Who am I? What is my purpose beyond the military?* I didn't have those answers.

I noticed one thing that stood out no matter where I ended up. People always wanted to open up and have a conversation with me. Co-workers would tell me their feelings and their struggles in life. It was a lot of 'couch' time, but I didn't mind. They saw me as someone who had a different perspective on life. They saw the drive I had to improve things, even if I didn't see it in myself. The more I connected with people, the more I felt good afterward. It was the same with customers. They would seem happy when I was able to assist them, but I could sense there was more going on beneath the surface. As much as I tried to help, I knew that saving them money on their purchase wasn't the solution in the grand scheme of things.

Over time, all the emotions and problems I had been ignoring kept pushing closer to the surface. I had suppressed so much because I didn't know how to let go of it. I didn't have time to think about how I felt because I was too busy making things happen. I continued to learn as I went from job to job, leveling up in titles. But something inside my heart was telling me, *You need to take care of you.* I didn't know exactly what that meant, at first. I thought it was maybe eating healthy or working out, so I started there. But, it grew into something deeper. At my lowest moments when I thought I couldn't do this anymore, something would tell me, *There's more for you ahead.*

The feeling of suspense was worse than the defeat of the rat race, so I started researching, eager to find 'more.' Every time I would reach some level of accomplishment, I would get distracted and start chasing 'Good Time Charlie.' I knew that partying wasn't the answer, but I did it anyway to escape reality and avoid dealing with my problems. My wife started noticing that I wasn't present all the time. I was gone... in my head, reliving the past. I was trying to get back to what was familiar while missing the life in front of me. We were having kids, and needed to come together as a team. We were not seeing eye to eye anymore and it was affecting our marriage.

Having a family made me realize that I needed to get my head out of my four-points-of-contact (my butt) and make some changes, or I wasn't going to be around for long. I was trying to get healthy, but I ended up just yo-yo-ing back and forth. I needed to do something. During my time in service, I experienced how difficult and unforgiving the world can be. It made me more protective of my family and I started questioning, *What am I doing?* Every time I would backslide, I would end up derailed. Then it occurred to me: *Maybe the best version of me is deeper than my physical self.*

My wife and I decided to go to church. That threw a monkey wrench in my gears, and launched me off the hamster wheel I'd been spinning on. Church made me stop and think, but not about me. It broke my routine from running on autopilot. It made me pause and think about Jesus. Even though I wasn't singing or putting my hands in the air, I was worshiping in my own way—whispering is still worship. As we went to church more often, I prayed more. I felt less focused on myself and a stronger connection with God.

A guest speaker at our church was talking about how we live in the past. When we get into a relationship, we carry our baggage with us. When we ask God for forgiveness and pray, "God help me," we put the baggage down. But as soon as we walk out of the church, we pick it up again and put it over our shoulders. We don't want it, but by keeping it we feel in control. Toward the end of the sermon, he said, "You know what? I just feel something pulling on my heart. I feel something calling me. There's someone in here that I'm really speaking to right now. Someone that was in the military. Someone that got medicaled out. Someone that was in the... ARMY!" I looked around, questioning, *Is he talking about ME?*

I live in a Marine town. There aren't too many Army guys here. When the speaker said, "This message is for *you*." I felt a jolt of shock, like there was a big neon arrow pointing right at me. I was like, "WHAT? Do you mean me?" I looked around, seeing everyone was fixated on the speaker; no one else appeared to be having the same reaction. I seemed to be the only one acknowledging that something more was going on, something higher than I could understand. I was puzzled and confused. I was sure about one thing, though; my life would never be the same again.

I had reached a point in my life where I was trying to control every aspect of my journey. I needed to have every answer to each of my life's scenarios. I would coordinate every move before me to the point where I was always a confused bundle of nerves. Then, I understood that the enemy wasn't on the outside. I was fighting a different battle, the one inside of me. That's why I had such a hard time. The enemy was aware of my weaknesses and waiting to ambush me at every turn. This internal danger was new territory to me; the enemy had always been external. I wasn't trained for this new inner feeling. I felt unprepared.

As I developed a better relationship with God, I started feeling powerful sensations in my body. My visions and dreams increased as I continued to pray more often. When these sensations first started to happen, I would get what felt like goosebumps x10. Like something bad was going to happen. It reminded me of Iraq, and it made me hyper-aware of my surroundings. The more I processed my emotions without anything bad happening, the more I realized God was leading me in a direction to discover more.

My wife and I started working on our relationship together. We figured out the areas that we needed to grow and decided the best direction for our family was to educate ourselves. We took a class that taught us how to work together financially. This gave me the freedom to leave my job. Something told me things were going to shift, and I needed to stay ahead of it. If we hadn't taken these first steps to improve our situation, I would have felt shackled to the job, unable to make that leap.

I began reading and searching for any explanation for what I was experiencing. *Why was I feeling these inner experiences? What's going on with all these visions?* Something told me to type "intuition coach" into the search bar. In the results, a course popped up, and I joined a *Called to Coach* workshop. It taught me how to use my intuition and explained what's been going on my whole life. Ever since I was a kid, I always could sense things on a different level. I didn't know exactly what these feelings were at the time, and I couldn't put my finger on them. We all have this ability; people call it gut instinct, intuition, and self-knowing, but there's a lot more to it. The workshop gave me the language to describe what I was feeling. As a guy, I was never confident enough to express what I was going through. The term "women's intuition" made me believe that this wasn't possible; that it was only for the ladies. Little did I know learning we all have the gift of intuition would open a huge can of worms.

As I started to acknowledge and identify my emotions, it brought up flashbacks from my past. These would repeat in my head—a little too often for my liking. I was confused, angry, and excited all at the same time. I knew what needed to be done. I knew I had to push forward, but it was hard to endure these surfacing emotions. I was reliving all my past experiences simultaneously. Once I had an idea of my intuition, I began blaming myself for not having this knowledge earlier. I was angry because if I had known more then my past would have looked different. The thought of avoiding all the pain I went through was defeating. The inner battle was getting real, and I didn't feel ready to continue.

One day, I decided to practice what I had learned. I stood in front of the mirror in my bedroom and began to pray and then stopped to listen. That's when I felt a wave of vibration throughout my entire body; I felt peace and serenity, then I saw an image of me floating into the sky. I had armor on, and above me was another person in armor with wings. I didn't quite see the face. It was just a bright light. As I floated up, I asked this image in front of me, "What's going on? Why am I here?"

He said, "You ready?"

I was confused. "What do you mean am I ready?"

He said, "Are you ready to help? Are you ready to serve?"

"What does that mean? Does that mean like a football coach or basketball coach? I don't understand what this whole thing is."

He told me that something was coming and I needed to be prepared for it. I needed to start growing and learning so I could help others. "The world is changing, and we need you to stand in victory. But first, you have to take those arrows out of you."

As I looked down at my body, I realized there were arrows sticking out of my torso. The image told me: "These arrows are all your blockages in life. They represent everything that is preventing you from reaching your full potential. You have to pull those arrows out yourself. Once you do, you're no longer shackled to the past. With each arrow you pull out, I'm going to help you release it. So, if you choose to put them back in, you can no longer blame your past because you'll be making the choice in the present."

At that moment, I felt a *release*, a *freedom*, a newfound *awareness* of who I could become. I understood that this was my mission and the path God gave me. My purpose was to serve and be the light to help guide others.

For a few days after that vision, I was on fire! I was feeling motivated, like someone pushed the factory reset button, and it felt good! Then, the arrows I had pulled out started poking at me again. My brother had taken his life a few years before. His passing was so hard on me because he was my little brother. It devastated me knowing that I helped stop soldiers from committing suicide in the military, but I wasn't able to help save my brother. *How could I be Called to Coach if I couldn't even save someone I loved?* I thought I was over the loss, but it hit me again. I felt so much defeat I went into another bout of depression. More and more unresolved emotional barriers showed up in every way. It felt like I got punched by an ultra-combo, just like in Street Fighter.

Yet, instead of being down in the dumps for weeks, I could bounce back quicker. The difference was, this time, I was connected to God. I continued to educate myself and work on my intuition. I furthered my research and learned about who I really was. I made progress in pinpointing the emotional experiences I was having. The guiding light within me started getting brighter. I could see my path, like someone walked into a dark room holding a lantern and turned up the dial to the highest setting. Suddenly, I could see more of what was in front of me. In the past, my guiding light would flicker, like someone was messing with a dimmer switch. As I continue to increase my intuitive awareness, I gain more insight into my purpose.

There are plenty of times in my story I could have checked out. But something deep inside of me said *You're not done. There's more to your journey.* That's when the light bulb turned on; I finally understood how it worked. When you pray, it's you talking to God. When you use your intuition, it's God speaking to you. It took me a while to learn that it's a 2-way street. If I wanted God to allow me to light my path and see where I was going, I needed to do my part. God was showing me my past so I could continue to grow. I learned that if you ignore your emotions, they will come back around and hit you again. You cannot carry all the burdens of life; you have to let go of what your arrows represent and understand why you're releasing them.

I had to put in the work to accept my self-realization and finally understand myself. Or as I like to call it—My Superpowers. Exactly 1 year after joining the *Called to Coach* workshop, I signed up for their entire course at ATMANA Academy. Since graduating as a Certified Intuitive Life Coach, it has become clear to me that my purpose and mission for God has always been to guide others to find their light and walk their path. As a Breakthrough Coach, I now help others identify their barriers and guide them to release their arrows. People still strike up conversations wherever I go, but now I embrace the opportunity to help others. *I am living on purpose.*

If you've ever heard that voice inside your head or felt the tingling sensation that there's more than meets the eye, listen to it! It could be guiding you toward your purpose. When you sit with yourself, reflect, and listen to what your heart is telling you, things will become more apparent. The light inside of you will shine so bright that it will reveal your path ahead. Embrace the changes you feel as you release the arrows of your past. You have the potential to become limitless. Your breakthrough is coming; follow your light!

IGNITE ACTION STEPS

- **Set aside time** in silence to consider where your arrows might be. Schedule a time without ANY distractions to reflect.

- **Determine the emotions** in your life that you carry around that you no longer want to. Decide on what needs to be released.

- **Give yourself permission** to understand the emotions surrounding the arrows you need to let go of. Ask yourself why you kept them and what purpose they serve. Do you still need them in your life?

- **Make a decision** to be aware of these emotions, so that when they creep up (because they will) you're able to recognize it and keep the arrows at bay.

Eric LG Longoria — United States of America
Breakthrough Coach
www.ericlgcoaching.com
lg.369ao
ericlgcoaching
eric-longoria-369ao11bg

IGNITE™
your
Purpose

Purpose Prompt 8

CREATE MEANING IN YOUR LIFE.

Purpose and meaning often go hand in hand. When we assign a positive meaning with a beneficial outcome, we feel purposeful. Bring meaning onto your day and take action that inspires you. Ask yourself:

What did I do today that felt meaningful?

_____

_____

_____

_____

_____

What can I do that is meaningful tomorrow?

_____

_____

_____

_____

_____

_____

What will give me meaning in the future?

_____

_____

_____

_____

_____

_____

_____

_____

_____

_____

_____

_____

_____

_____

_____

Loretta Mitchell

Loretta Mitchell

"Life's about changes; welcome new beginnings."

All human beings have meaning and purpose. We are all pieces of a giant puzzle, and all pieces of that puzzle are necessary to complete the picture of our lives. See the joy in your life daily as you seek the passion that fulfills your soul. Go about life as best you can without the fear of loss or the worry that your life will one day end. Death is inevitable, so why not live? I encourage you to fully immerse yourself in living the life you desire and know that your life is divinely purposeful.

Her Own Calling

As a child, I seemed to have one *purpose*: playing. I enjoyed my dolls, farm toys, books, and the playmates that my neighborhood supplied. First thing in the morning, I would go outside to see who was around to join in a game of tag or hide-and-seek. There were usually three or four kids to hang out with and find some fun. Even if no one was around, I had my imagination to help me live my purpose.

One beautiful sunny day, I pedaled my tricycle with my 5-year-old legs up to my favorite spot: my neighbor's hilly front yard. On that particular day, as I stared at the fluffy clouds above me, an awareness that I was becoming older sank in. I was outgrowing my beloved tricycle, and I felt taller perched on that mountain top. For a brief moment, while looking up at the sky, I wondered what life was all about and what I was here for. I felt a strong presence of a Higher Power. That moment stuck with me as I resumed my childhood adventures for the day.

As I grew older, my purpose continued, and I had a great upbringing enjoying my life. My family overcame their challenging start in Canada as my parents were immigrants from Germany post World War II. My mom and dad wanted a peaceful and happy life and were determined to give us every opportunity to experience the best that they could offer. I knew I could not live in their home forever, and by the time I graduated, I began to face my future. My parents wished for me to attend university, particularly my mother. I willingly agreed as that appeared to be a logical direction for me.

In choosing my path, I greatly admired my high school physical education teacher. She was an intelligent, effective teacher with a lovely sense of humor who could teach sports without portraying the typical *jock* image. I wanted to be like her. I decided to attend the university in the nearest city to earn my degree specializing in physical education. I was encouraged to follow that path as I excelled in sports and was reasonably academic during my high school years.

I quickly became accustomed to the university and big city lifestyle, and found I could easily make friends. I lived in the university residence during my first year. As a welcoming gift to the entire all-female ninth floor, we were given a T-shirt with the words, *Each of Us Has Her Own Calling.* It was a nice gift, but I had never thought about a purpose or a passion, never mind a *calling.* I was years away from comprehending the meaning of those powerful life concepts.

Despite my original passion for physical education, within my first semester, I was forced to reconsider my path and my purpose. I developed a physical condition that compromised my ability to complete the active and physical components required for my chosen major. I wondered whether to switch majors entirely and worried about wasting time and money or letting my supportive parents down; I filled my extra class options with subjects that made me happy and intrigued, not giving much thought to whether they would prepare me for my future career.

Through it all, my boyfriend (my best friend who became my husband) remained my biggest supporter, saying, "Do whatever it is you want to do." In contrast to my wavering interests, he knew what he wanted to do and used his abilities to pursue physically demanding work rather than academics. He was willing to support both of us in our newly married life. I completed my Bachelor of Education degree and moved to a small northern community where my young husband was happily employed as a truck driver in the oil patch. I was mapping out the next steps of my purpose.

I was elated when I was quickly hired to teach at the elementary/middle school. Life looked extremely promising for both me and my husband. He jumped right into the oilfield business and bought himself a brand-new truck. I, on the other hand, started off doing great but soon began to feel the challenges of my chosen career. I enjoyed the students, devoting many hours to creating lessons and learning more about the subjects I had to teach. Yet, I found that I was somewhat sensitive to the criticism I was receiving and began floundering in my ability to maintain control or enforce any effective discipline.

Although I had a well-rounded background with children through babysitting, teaching swimming lessons, and Sunday school, I was not prepared for the problems I was facing. My teaching peers were encouraging during that time, but I was not given positive support from the administration. The principal did not know what to do with the students I had issues with. Fresh out of university, I was not wise enough to know how to effectively deal with problems and stay on my purpose path.

My first year of teaching ended, and I was not given a contract for the next year. I had never experienced anything like what I was going through. I was angry at the administration. I was hurt and humiliated for what I saw as unjustified. I was embarrassed to tell anyone, including my family, about my situation. It was a huge blow to my ego. My self-worth and self-esteem disappeared. I had to dig deep to give myself uplifting pep talks as the negative internal dialogue easily took over. During this time of deep despair, I began a new quest for the purpose of my life.

Since we resided in an isolated community, I could not look for another teaching job without relocating. It was time for me to take a break, and I became the chief support for my husband and his trucking career. It was time to pursue *his* dream.

Within the next year, we shifted directions; we found a trucking company that would give us a job to see North America together as a driving team. That meant I had to acquire my truck driving license. Learning how to drive an 18-wheeler and the comprehensive driving test was more challenging and stressful than 4 years of university.

We were able to work together 24/7, get paid while traveling, and see a lot of the country. My husband taught me to drive that truck so I could navigate all manner of roads and highways. We spent the next seven years driving our semi on the highway with a couple of seasons of hauling locally so we could stay closer to home.

We were extremely fortunate to see the beauty and bounty of our country, building relationships with the people we encountered. I was both impressed and humbled by the people we met. Folks from all walks of life joined the transportation community: university-educated, life-educated, Vietnam veterans, farmers, and husband/wife duos like us. Anyone could be a truck driver if that's what they desired. Those traveling years provided me with a whole new perspective on my life. I had found purpose in helping others, sharing stories, and forming friendships.

After a number of years living on the road, I decided I had had enough bouncing around in the truck. I longed for a home, family, and a more 'normal' life. We decided we would both retire from the highway trucking life, and we would find a new way of making a livelihood. After our years of traveling, I was excited to step into the world of motherhood. I was looking forward to the day I would be called *Mommy*. Having children was an important goal in my life and one I am thankful that I was able to accomplish.

Our first child, Heather, was born, followed by our son, Jesse. I was a fully engaged stay-at-home mom and volunteered in whatever my children were involved with. Being with my kids during their early childhood allowed me ample time to get to know each of them. I enjoyed the lifestyle that being an at-home mom provided. Despite all the jobs associated with children and household duties, I was feeling my own pressure that I needed to do more. I was questioning my purpose, who I was, and feeling a lack of self-worth because I was not employed. Sadly, many stay-at-home moms face this dilemma. So, I officially placed my name on the substitute teaching list.

Soon enough, my new career as a professional *sub* teacher began, along with my prime role as a mother and household manager. That new direction started when both my kids were under the age of 3. I averaged teaching one day per week. That gave my kids a chance to playdate with some neighborhood children. The balance of work and home life was a comfortable fit for our family at first.

Life has a way of throwing us in a new direction. The school I spent most of my time subbing at was closing at the end of Heather's grade one year, right as I surprisingly found myself pregnant with baby number 3. I returned to being a full-time stay-at-home mom. Upon reflection, I am glad I was able to devote time to our new little guy. We both benefitted, and so did my family. My husband and I knew how precious my time at home would be for everyone.

Quickly my kids were growing up, and I felt I had to get serious about a *career* path, believing my career was tied to my purpose in the world. I had already begun parent volunteering in my kids' school over the years and I was given the opportunity to become a teacher assistant for a couple of terms. Soon enough, I stepped back into substitute teaching. I enjoyed the job most days, although juggling family and work was quite hectic at that time in my life. But being busy wasn't the worst thing I would soon be dealing with. My purpose was to change and shake the entire foundation of all that I had built.

No sooner had I stepped back into the working world as a substitute teacher when life took a sudden, unexpected turn in the most unwelcome direction. On August 28, 2004, my Seventeen-year-old daughter died suddenly in a vehicle accident 2 days before her first day of broadcasting school. Nothing could prepare me for the sorrow and heartache that my daughter's death created. Maybe if I'd had a *real job,* I would have pulled myself together, but I did not *have* to return to substitute teaching. I called it quits. Heather's departure deserved some heartfelt contemplation. I felt a need to take time for myself and fortunately had the support of my family as they too needed assistance with their grieving process. I was on a mission to find answers to my many questions about life and death. One which was; *Why did she have to go?*

I immersed myself in the spiritual world and all things metaphysical and mystical. While attending a *Signature Cell Healing* workshop, Rev. Mel Morishige introduced me to the Great Awakening and to who we, as humans, are in the Universe. I discovered that we all have Divinity within us and that precious information has been withheld intentionally. I learned about ascension and how it is up to each one of us to raise our frequency by becoming conscious creators. That was the beginning of the knowledge that I was about to *re-learn* and when my greater purpose became more defined.

After a lifetime of seeking my path, following my husband's steadfast focus, and dedicating myself to my kids, I was finally aware of who I was meant to be for the greater good and the wider world. My purpose became clear; *I am here to support humanity's transition during the shift to higher consciousness.* I finally felt this was the clarity I was searching for. I was looking for healing and found my calling! My purpose was revealed.

After the event and alone in my hotel room, the tears flowed for several hours until it hurt so much I had to stop crying. I connected to the intense pain and sorrow of all I had lost; my beautiful daughter, other family members who unexpectedly passed, and who I was as a teacher, mother, wife, and friend. I embraced the realization that there *is* a greater plan. This was a huge epiphany for me. All things happen as they should. There is a purpose in everything, and I have a role in my life and the lives of others. I knew at that moment that all that I had been through was part of a master plan, guiding me to find a deeper meaning. It all felt clear, there is no loss. You never truly lose anyone or anything, circumstances just move you into a new direction, to be *in* purpose.

It was in that beautiful awareness that I felt my daughter's encouraging words, "You can do it, Mom." Instantly, I was ignited!

Hearing her words helped me see that life is truly precious *and* divine. I knew without a doubt that we all have meaning, direction, and purpose. The Universe has a grand plan and a great connectedness for all of us. I realized that by searching for the answers I had found and the greatest gift I would ever need, I finally felt my purpose blossoming inside of me.

Since that memorable day, I have been guided to continue taking steps into the unfamiliar. This information and internal knowing have been reaffirmed by the Kryon Family of spiritual teachers and guides that I now study with, along with other teachings that I have been encouraged to learn.

Becoming a Reiki Master/Teacher has allowed me to support others open to healing and awakening. Adding to doing energy work, I am now a host for the Stargate Circles, which is connected to the Stargate Experience Academy. During our online gatherings, we are creating a community of people from around the world connecting through high vibrational meditations and devoted to living in our purpose.

I encourage you, the reader, to step outside your comfort zone and search with all your heart, your mind, and your soul to find your divine purpose. As we raise our individual and collective consciousness, we *RealEyes*™ that we are One. Each action will lead you to your Calling. Your purpose is right in front of you.

IGNITE ACTION STEPS

These empowering words are significant to my life's purpose. I want to share them here to inspire you... Taken from Matthew 7:7 from the Holy Christian Bible:

1. **Ask, and it shall be given to you.** This is a very important step, as you must be careful of what you *wish* for. Your answer may not be immediate as it is all about timing. Be grateful to God for listening.

2. **Seek, and you will find.** When you look for direction, you will find clues to help you. You may discover a particular book or a class, or a travel adventure that you may be inspired to take. You may see signs from nature; a significant bird, the shape of a cloud, a penny from heaven, number patterns, or a message from a friend or even a stranger. Have gratitude for the signs you receive.

3. **Knock, and the door will be opened to you.** Once you take that first step, God will guide you on your path. When you are in alignment with your soul purpose, the doors will open for you. The Universe is cheering you on, be grateful for the opportunities that are presented to you.

Loretta Mitchell — Canada
Reiki Master/Teacher, Author, Speaker
www.balance4life.ca
Balance 4 Life (Alternative & Holistic Health Services)

Belinda Lee Schroeder

BELINDA LEE SCHROEDER

"If you get stuck on your path, dance the rest of the way."

Dear reader, my hope is that you will be inspired to not only want the best for yourself but be willing to Ignite your life from the purest joy that comes from within; when you follow your true purpose. This is not something elusive but rather something you've had all along. Just as Dorothy in *The Wizard of Oz* was searching for something she thought she didn't have, all of her trials and tribulations led her back home, where her truth was to begin with. Some of us are born going after our dreams right out of the cradle. However, we are all born *knowing* our dreams. Often, life gets in the way, and our gaze shifts to other sparkly things or difficult circumstances that consume our attention. Whatever path life has taken you on, YOU are worth finding. If you listen to your heart, you will remember who you are and your true purpose.

KEEP DANCING

I've questioned what my purpose is in so many ways it's ridiculous. The truth is, the day I stood by my little brother's casket gave me everything I ever needed to know, but I didn't recognize it at the time. That loss was so huge that I was terrified of losing love again, so my solution was to love others as much as possible. As a broken-hearted child, I believed I had to care for and protect everyone close to me.

Standing in the silence of that little sunroom in the funeral home, I felt a beautiful presence. I can still see Brian's angelic face looking as though he might smile at any moment. He was 4; I was thirteen. Leukemia was his battle, and he fought courageously. I feel that he knew who he was and why he was here. His life gifted all of us in our family with the greatest reminder to *remember to love each other no matter what.*

As the light streamed into that tiny room, I felt the presence of love, the presence of safety, and foreverness. It was a lot for a thirteen-year-old to process, but somehow I felt I could trust the things I believed in no matter what. And that the spirit that held my brother's hand and mine in those difficult moments assured me I would be okay.

It was late summer, and returning to junior high school, my heart was raw from losing my brother. I was feeling vulnerable and wanted to be invisible. The boys in the neighborhood had other ideas. They would rush out in the morning and just *happen* to be on the sidewalk in front of my house as I emerged from my front door. "Can I walk you to school?" said a boy with a wide grin that made me slightly uncomfortable. At first, I wanted to avoid this new attention. As time went on, however, I decided I would choose who got my attention, not them. I tried to stay open to their interest as it reduced my loneliness. Eventually, I became obsessed, or "boy crazy," as various family members would say of me throughout my teens.

Looking to make sense of all that had happened to my brother, I searched for answers in new-age bookstores. Despite myself, I never lost touch with the world beyond. The sense of Spirit was always by my side. At some point, I realized that the boys, while fun, were not filling that space in my heart that was still aching.

I was grateful that we were moving when I started high school, and I took the opportunity to begin a new path of discovery through my love of Dance. Even though I had been dancing since I was a young girl, something inside me began to recognize that for me, dancing was a way that I could connect with Spirit. I set up a dance troupe, and no matter my other commitments, I would dance. It also gave me a way to grieve or feel comfort from whatever teenage storm was happening in school.

For years I was still carrying that thirteen-year-old, broken-hearted child of myself around, only to realize there wasn't much chance that I could really receive love except through my love of Dance. When I was creating a dance piece, I felt the exhilaration of experiencing everything and nothing all at once, being transcended. At the end of the day, after a beautiful mix of writing the movements and dancing them out, I would collapse on the floor full of smiles as though Spirit was there on the floor next to me, smiling back at the pure joy of exhaustion. I felt Spirit alive and well right by my side.

With my connection to Spirit strong, I took a chance and eventually married and had a son. The marriage didn't last, but the joy of raising my 2-year-old son and continuing to dance did! I built a dance studio in our little apartment, and we both enjoyed it. We would blast the music and have fun, silly dancing. I thought I would be a dancer and a choreographer, and I was supposed to do that with my life.

During that time, I used Dance as a means of self-care. To expand my dancing, I began to do yoga and meditation before and after my dancing. I increasingly realized that Dance was like a love language between me and Spirit.

Years later, when I married for the second time, I returned to a local dance program to take choreography classes. I enrolled in twenty hours of dance classes a week. I was feeling that familiar high of joyful movement.

This was until one day in class, I heard a crunch in my knee as I turned in circles across the room. The gleeful smile on my face quickly turned to tears as I did everything possible to hit the floor gracefully. I tried to stand and quickly realized that wasn't happening. My mind shut down as my body went into shock. All I could think of was, *am I going to fail the class*? *How could I have missed that step? What will happen to the performance?* Despite my worries, they brought in a medic, and I was taken to the hospital.

After seeing the doctor, he delivered the news that I should stop dancing because the cartilage had become soft in my knee and joints. The reason for this was because I had become pregnant, unbeknownst to me.

I was always good at pivoting. I threw myself into having a new baby that was coming into my life, knowing how much I already loved being a mother. When the doctor said, "No more dancing," however, I heard, "No more passion." For me, Dance was Spirit. I almost felt like I would have to break up with Spirit. Even though some part of me knew that wasn't entirely true, I still felt lt. I wondered, did this mean my purpose wasn't really going to be Dance? I was thirty-three years old, and I knew that I had to make peace with my dancing in whatever form it might take in the future. However, I could feel a dark sadness pulling me into resignation.

August 1st was coming up, the anniversary of my Brother's passing. I would take my son to visit my parents and my sister in New Jersey. I first went to the doctor to verify that I could travel due to my pregnancy. While waiting for the doctor to come into the room, I noticed a piece of art with a verse from the book of Samuel. I loved it so much that I decided I would name my new baby Samuel Joseph, as I felt instinctively he was a boy.

I was relieved that the doctor said all was well to travel because it had been eleven years since I'd had a baby. With excitement to see my family, I packed up my son, Aaron, and we headed to New Jersey. I could see the joy that Aaron was feeling as he shared his future plans for his baby sibling. He kept leaning in from the back seat as he said, "Mom, we have to get him some Transformers®!" or, "What other kinds of toys do you think we should get?" I could see that big-brother smile on his face as he relaxed back into his seat.

As we drove the New Jersey turnpike, a driver in a small, dark sports car came up fast behind me, recklessly cutting me off and causing me to jerk the steering wheel. At that moment, adrenaline took over as I realized this distraction had put me in a place where I had to cross several lanes quickly. Mindful of my son in the back, and my pregnant belly pushing against the seatbelt; I swerved too far and landed on the shoulder. I was shaken and scared as I felt a pain in my belly, a strain.

A policeman stopped and got us back to where we needed to be. I pressed on with my drive, trying not to worry Aaron with the inner fears I felt. We finally arrived in Sparta, a beautiful lake community that my parents had recently moved to. I was feeling wiped out and went up to bed. The following day I wasn't feeling right, and we decided to run to the local hospital to ensure everything was okay. I had a sonogram, and I could see Samuel's heartbeat. I went home relieved. The following day, I heard gleeful whooping from Aaron. My parents had already made breakfast and were preparing the boat to take Aaron water skiing. I decided not to go, and my sister opted to stay home with me. We had a great lake view and could watch all the fun. I could hear Aaron all the way up to the house, "Look, Mom!" as he took his first water skiing lesson.

Suddenly, as I stood up, I felt a warm rush of blood and knew instantly that it wasn't good. Amanda was only seventeen, but she took matters into her hands. She kept a calm, steady voice, saying, "It's okay. You're okay." I was scared. Everyone else was out on the boat. I got into bed and despaired as my body contracted for hours in pain. I knew that I was losing the baby. She stayed by my side and talked me through the pain. In those moments, I didn't feel Spirit. I didn't feel anything. I was empty. I ended up back at the hospital that night, and it was confirmed I had lost the baby. I cried all the way home.

When I told Aaron, he was silent. He didn't really want to speak of it, and I truly understood his pain. When you lose a child, whether it's your own child or sibling, it leaves a hole in your being. And perhaps we spend too much time trying to figure out how to make it better when we really can't. All we can do is look ahead into the light where love resides.

I took the time I needed to process my loss. I decided to go to the beach for some downtime. That would bring about some introspection as to what was next. One morning, I was standing in the cold wet sand as the sun was rising majestically over the dark and perfect ocean. Its fluffy white wave tips caught the first light rays, quickly illuminating an ideal stream of water before me. It was spectacular. I couldn't even speak. At some point, I asked the ocean, almost embarrassingly, "What is my purpose?"

Even though that's what I'd walked down to the water's edge to ask, it almost seemed ridiculous as I was standing in awe of such power and eternal beauty. Yet, like many of us, I began to forget the moment and returned to my need to know: *Who am I? What am I here to do?* I heard my heart respond, "Does it matter? Are you happy right now?" *Yes*, I answered tentatively. "Well then, just be, just enjoy, get so present that you feel this experience!"

What did the ocean answer back? She didn't. She just continued her steady rhythm that I knew was eternal; that experience I also recognized in my heartbeat and the breath I was drawing. I realized that these are the things I can count on no matter what.

I suddenly remembered that while I was having a sonogram of Samuel in the hospital, I had asked the nurse what the blinking light was on the screen. She said, "That is your son's heartbeat." Remembering that, I wept tears into the waves washing over my feet. I had not only seen his heartbeat, but I had the gift of feeling his love as well. He truly touched my heart.

As time went on, holding that sweet memory in my mind, I came to a place of peace with the child in me who lost her brother so many years before. When she gets scared that she might be alone forever, I remind her that she is *never* alone. None of us are truly alone because when we are brave enough to open ourselves to love, then we can feel the love we have from within. I was brave enough to let love in for my new son, and I still feel him all around me. By loving him, I feel all the love that is within me and the eternal love that is always present.

I found that my purpose is to love... simply that, each and every day. The precious, gentle, innocent love my brother instilled in me has reminded me of my true purpose and to never give up on love. I often feel the energy of my son Samuel reminding me to go for joy and to Keep Dancing!

I had 2 daughters not long after, and soon life became busy raising my family. My life continued to take me to more studies about spirituality, meditating more deeply and understanding my connection to Spirit. My desires shifted as my family grew up, and soon I began to feel the pull to serve as my future self whispered, "Time for what is next." I went off to get a Ph.D. in Alternative and Complementary Medical Therapies. I now help others discover *their* true purpose.

I realized that the most important thing is never to lose that joy that comes from expressing our desires because that Spirit exists through us. The calling of Spirit will never go away. It's as though Spirit heard all of my longings from when I was a child, through all of the difficulties of life and all of the yearnings. As promised, Spirit never forgot me.

Now I experience staying in the truest essence of myself; that is where I find my true purpose. I didn't return to dancing in the way I had wanted. It took a long time to allow that love back into my life. Yet my beating heart reminds me I can dance to express the joy that comes from my own self-love! Everything I have manifested here on earth has come as a result of the magnificent love I allow to flow through me.

For as long as humans have walked the earth, I know in my soul we've been asking *What is my purpose?* That elusive question we seem to feel must be answered if we are to create a path toward our destiny. But what if your purpose was just to be?

What if your purpose was just to wake up in this moment and let the impulse of what you want to do in the moment without judgment from others be your path?

What if you could still be loved, accepted, and not judged because you stop doing, and doing, and doing... and instead took a risk and did what you desired?

What do you truly love?

What will make you want to dance?

Allow love in and let it lead you to your true Purpose.

IGNITE ACTION STEPS

- **Be Still:** Take time daily to be still, whether you find stillness in sitting with your eyes closed, walking in nature, or riding a bike. Give your brain a break and clear your mind. You will find it easier to connect to your Spirit if you can settle your thoughts.

- **Be Listening:** Don't be afraid to ask questions. Spirit is always giving us answers; we just have to listen.

- **Believe:** Opening your heart to trust yourself is probably the most important step to opening yourself to transformation and manifestation.

- **Be Free:** Permit yourself to do the things you love. Allow the joy that comes from actually doing this. Note how you feel, and remember that you want more of that!

- **Be You:** This may seem obvious given the above steps, and may appear as though it would be an easy 1,2,3, and then you're free! However, it does take time to unwind things from your past. The good news is that it is possible and attainable to heal those things and achieve freedom. It is up to you to decide when you want to experience the truth, the freedom, and the joy that *is* you.

Belinda Lee Schroeder, PhD — United States of America
www.belindaleeschroeder.com
belindaleeschroeder@gmail.com
belinda.schroeder

Purpose Prompt 9

PURPOSE-DRIVEN REFLECTION

Reflecting on your day can help define your purpose; use these reflective questions below to help you find meaning in your purpose.

What did I do today that aligned with my purpose and goals?

_____

_____

_____

_____

_____

What did I do today that sparked joy?

_____

_____

_____

_____

_____

_____

How can I work on fulfilling my purpose every day?

_____

_____

_____

_____

_____

_____

_____

_____

_____

_____

_____

_____

_____

_____

_____

Lorena Lee

Lorena Lee

"Through stillness, darkness, and the unknown, you find your true self."

My intention is to *illuminate*. Illuminate the uncomfortable dark spaces we may be avoiding and provoke new thought patterns around them. Illuminate curiosity. Illuminate worth, trust, and PURPOSE. Let's normalize the unknown and embrace the ride, feeling safe in acknowledging its illumination and power. I want you to know that your purpose is being open-minded and doesn't need to be clearly defined or boxed. Purpose comes in waves for some and may be as still as a beautiful lake at sunset for others; as long as it nourishes you... purpose just may be the gift of life.

Unboxed

Illuminate the Unknown

What are you going to be when you grow up? I always dreaded that age-old question as a child. To avoid the awkward response of "I don't know," I would have an answer preloaded to avoid disappointment. "Uhhh... an emergency room doctor." That seemed like a winner for the receiving end as they enjoyed a vision of me that brought notoriety and wealth. Don't get me wrong, I may have had a slight addiction to watching trauma and ER shows and could completely envision taking that path. Yet, life had other plans for me because my path was never meant to be as the crow flies. I had to own the truth that I didn't, and might never, clearly understand my purpose.

Illuminate Rest

Time off. The outside programming and societal pressure were heavy during my upbringing. There is a stigma that when we leave high school, you must know where you are going and what you will be. I enjoy doing things my way (ask any of my family members, and they'll tell you). Against popular convention, I chose to take a break after high school. I was told I would never go to college if I did so, that I would lose interest and never want to advance my education further. But I had already proven I wasn't one to follow the beaten path. I took a year off to enjoy my favorite places and people. Long days under the sun with friends on the lake. Late evenings, basking under the moonlight, listening to nature, exercising daily, and putting my health first. Not to mention saving extra money to prepare for launching into my next adventure.

I gathered many moments of silence during that time, whether I was reading or simply meditating. An unsuspecting friend recommended a book that he felt was awakening. I knew if this book was impactful for *him,* I needed to take note, as he doesn't share deep thoughts often. I basically ran to get my hands on it. It was called "A New Earth" by Eckhart Tolle. Boy, was he right. That was my jumping-off point for opening my mind to different ways of thinking. From there, I dove into a personal journey, researching many religions and ways of thought. After my year off to reset and enjoy some downtime, I was more ready than ever to start college and sink further into academia with a newfound thirst for being engulfed in learning.

Illuminate the Mind

Dentistry. At the time, I was working at a dental office, plugging away through community college coursework. Deep down inside, I always wanted to be a psychologist and help people in need, as the human mind and interaction fascinated me. I just couldn't get out of my head the pressure of letting all those people down who were expecting me to be a doctor or something note-worthy. "Psychology and counseling doesn't pay well, Lorena. Are you sure that is the path you want to take?" Man, did I fall for that spiel! It felt terrible progressing forward on a career path of medical prerequisites with my inner knowing screaming it wasn't the direction I was supposed to be headed. Since I was gaining experience and under the supervision of an amazing dentist who inspired me, I decided to switch focus (and compromise again) to take courses toward dental school. Since I was achieving high grades, I convinced myself that everything was going swimmingly and I must have been on the right trajectory.

Illuminate the Heart

Love. Then I met him, a US Marine: charismatic, driven, and loving. It was at a classmate's graduation party when we first collided. He was home for a short while between assignments. The first night, we sat on a curb until the sun came up, talking about life. We didn't want it to end. We flowed effortlessly together, and our connection was undeniable. Within months, we were engaged. Unbeknownst to me, this connection would align my life path in a way I could have never imagined.

That relationship led us through multiple overseas deployments and unstable emotional territory, an absolute whirlwind. Sadness, loneliness, frustration, excitement, and worry are just a fraction of the emotions I felt during that time. I witnessed first-hand the effects on both the deployed service members and the people back home supporting their loved ones. It wasn't long after a few rotations of being with and away from one another that I realized things were not quite the same. The distance brought out a lot of insecurities and instability in our commitment to one another. Leaning on unhealthy vices to cope eventually got the best of us. That was a pivotal point for me. After many years of fighting to regain what we once had, it all fell apart. It's something that still shakes me up many years later. I felt helpless; I couldn't even help the one I loved the most.

Despite the long-lasting pain that ending brought, it was the beginning of clarifying my boundaries and determining my own path, even if it wasn't a clear one. I decided nobody would influence my mind and heart any longer, and I would indeed switch my major and focus on a career rooted in supporting others: Psychology. I always wanted to help anyone I could through challenging times. It may have been an unpopular choice, but I was not letting anyone stop me. Thankfully, I found a program to intertwine into my life while I continued toward many goals.

Illuminate fear

Shows and events. A fellow coworker shared, "Lorena, I have a friend that works in automotive. She goes to shows and special events, and I think you would be great for it." I am a huge supporter of not closing doors on opportunities even when it is not on your intended path. Which means, of course, I took the interview! Gratefully, it went fantastically. That new job as a Product Specialist afforded me the ability to see the country and meet new people. *Yes, please!*

The only downfall: I was terrified of public speaking... a requirement for the job. I remembered long ago, a psychic in my small town said to me, "Your experiences are building your future, and you will be talking to the masses someday. It is part of your PURPOSE." HA! At the time, you could not pay me a million dollars to stand up in front of people and speak. The sheer thought of having a spotlight on me and hearing my voice reverberate through a room with people staring at me was petrifying. With all those eyes on me, I could feel my heart race just thinking about it. But I took the job anyway.

Illuminate Others

Social Work. Well, here we go again, another shift in academic direction. *Surprise, surprise.* Psychology wasn't the best fit anymore, as the flexibility post-graduation for employment options felt limited. I needed to hone in on a topic that was relatable to me, as I felt sharing my own experiences may be beneficial to others. Having an understanding of deployments and their underlying impact piqued my interest. I found that the University of Southern California had a highly acclaimed Master's program in Military and Veterans Affairs, which gave me the chance to still travel for work and complete my degree at the same time. My workload was overwhelming at times. But I knew nothing compares to those who fought for our freedoms and were struggling as they returned home only to find themselves in a continuous battle. Wanting to support them kept me humble and motivated.

Illuminate Darkness

Death. I have always been afraid of death. Surely, from a selfish standpoint, if I dig into it. Numerous questions ruminate in my mind. *What am I missing? Where am I going? Did I fulfill my purpose? What am I leaving behind?* It wasn't until the passing of my Aunt Lorena, my namesake, that it all changed. I was in my late 20s at the time and navigating religious and spiritual confusion. My Aunt Lorena, "Queenie Renie," had been fighting a rare bone cancer, multiple myeloma, for far too many years. *She was worn out and depleted.* It was her choice to return home to be surrounded by loved ones while in hospice care. Family and friends comforted her through the days, and my mother and I decided that we would not leave her alone at night, as one of us was always standing guard at her bedside. She would have tremors and moans that would crush our souls. We wanted her to experience no pain and have a peaceful disconnection from this world. When she would appear unsettled, we'd hold her hand, rub her legs, or talk to her. We noticed that when we did that, she would relax and quiet down. That is where the illumination in darkness began to arise for me as the transformation was happening through the most painful times.

Illuminate Time

Time. Aunt Lorena had an antique grandfather clock that would chime every 15 minutes—a sound I will never forget. Her moments of audible discomfort would chime in just like that damn clock. As we slept on the floor next to her, we would wake as she moved or made a noise to put our hands on her until she'd calm down again. The irony of that clock still gets me to this day. Time is constructed, yet we toss it around as if it's always going to exist.

It was mid-afternoon on a cold winter day, and the sunlight was illuminating her sunroom, where she chose to rest. The unknown darkness of death hovered and would take over our thoughts. Is it minutes away or days? Sadly, that afternoon, it was minutes; her time had come to transition into the next realm. I witnessed something I have never seen in my life. I saw her spirit leave her body. As she took her last breath, her eyes followed what seemed to be a light; everything relaxed, and she finally looked peaceful. At that moment, speechless, I knew there was something far bigger than this reality. Her soul was somewhere else, and her body was a shell right in front of me. The deep spirit connection had separated from this Earthly realm. I still talk to her these days. I sense she isn't as far away as many may believe, and in *time,* we will be reunited again.

Illuminate Touch

Reiki. Reiki uses gentle touch to help guide energy through the body that promotes balance and healing. I didn't know this at the time; I just knew something was working through me to ease the imbalance in others and myself, including my Aunt Renie. I felt my hands illuminate; they felt a sensation they had never experienced before; it was electric. It was as if I was able to touch or hover over an area and create a healing heat that moved energy around for the greatest good. When signs come in repetition for me, I like to take notice as I believe in synchronicity. I heard the call toward reiki 3 times from different people over the course of a couple of years. Okay, Universe, I hear you. I found an open-minded reiki master to guide me, and I completed my reiki master coursework. It was a clear alignment for me toward my deeper purpose.

Illuminate Sound

Sound. Energy and movement led me to many wonderful people. At a personal reiki session, the practitioner used sound as part of her modality. I could sense stress melting away as I dove deeper into hearing each sound, specifically connecting with its resonance. My scientific mind wanted to know more, yet my spiritual side said just follow the ease and flow. I was immediately drawn to singing bowls, a tool used for sound healing. Each bowl holds a different frequency and has the potential to balance and unwind inconsistencies within the body and energetic field. Admittedly, I made an impulse purchase and ordered a set of singing bowls and entwined them into my practice instantly. Sound therapy adds another dimension to a reiki session or spiritual practice. Through sound, I was able to tap into another level of my own consciousness. *Side of purpose, coming right up.*

Illuminate Truth

Abrupt change. After a wild few years navigating the pandemic with a job that was contingent on traveling, I was ready for change. An opportunity arose for a remote position that provided more stability and time at home. It sounded divine. The Universe felt differently. After a few months in, successfully learning and completing benchmarks, I noticed this inner feeling that someone was dissatisfied with my accomplishments. I sensed some colleagues did not have my best interests in mind and were projecting onto me their unhappiness. Sure enough, my gut feeling was right, and we abruptly parted ways, leaving me at a loss for words. I'd never had something end negatively in my career, and I truly didn't understand why until further review. What I did know was this: *I seek truth.* After illuminating the inconsistencies and circumstances, I quickly realized it was a blessing. The following weeks brought the most fruitful and exciting opportunities. That unexpected completion promptly turned into an uplifting, supported, and bountiful future.

Illuminate Opportunity

Author. I have written in the past, but surely not published work. Uncertainty and disbelief in myself crept in. If I was preaching to others about seizing opportunity, I could not slam the door on being published when it arrived. The process proved to be uncomfortable and overwhelming, paired with notes of insecurity. *Just my type of deep challenge.* We all have stories to tell, and it is never known who yours may inspire or motivate. So here I am, disconnected from my normal day-to-day workload to tap into the unknown and write about myself, which is the hardest part of it all. I trust in Source along the way to guide me, and it hasn't let me astray yet, as I am naturally attracted to abundance and getting outside of my comfort zone.

Illuminate the Power of Influence

Public Speaking. The psychic was right, after all. Most days, I spend a large portion of my career speaking to groups of people, facilitating training, and motivating teams and individuals toward next-level success. And they *do* pay me for it (though not a million dollars, per se), but when you are doing something you love, it is priceless. I didn't believe the psychic back then, and some days, I still don't believe it today. All of the transitions, jumps, dips, and pivots have brought me to right where I am supposed to be.

I know there is more in store for me as I continue to shift, learn, and grow. By keeping an open mind and limitless belief in my potential, it furthers my expansion. It makes me laugh thinking of all the days I would get up on stage to speak... only to turn around and walk right back down, terrified and tongue-tied. Or even worse, practice for weeks to prepare just to get up and freeze midway through. It was mortifying, but I never gave up believing in myself and believing in the power of communication. I know that by being consistent, I am creating my foundation of influence, which feels purposeful.

Illuminate Individuality

Voices. I contemplated not including this, but magically, there is space for it. I hear voices, yes, you heard that right. I do. I can remember falling asleep as a young child, hiding under the covers, frightened because I could hear communication outside myself as I drifted to sleep. I also had an all-knowing on topics I should not be tuned into. It wasn't odd for me to hear growing up that I was an "old soul" or "wise beyond my years." I understand now what I didn't then. I have been guided the *entire* time. (I know it is weird for some to hear, feel, or believe any of this—I accept that.) Proudly guided by something outside of myself, and I am not "crazy." I cannot scientifically describe all of the coincidences or connections I forge either. I used to be terrified of it and shut it out, but that served me or, more importantly, others no benefit. Now, I find calm knowing there is something much more vast and beautiful outside of this physical reality.

Whatever your gifts may be, be open to them. Explore and see where it leads you, even if others don't understand or support it. I now embrace my quirks and value those voices.

Illuminate Community
Community. Without the support of others, I would cease to exist. Through all of these transitions, it has been the love of others (and self) that guided me through. Whether it be a career shift or a death in the family, there is always an *illuminating* opportunity embedded somewhere. A couple of years ago, during my grandmother Memes' last moments on this Earth, I was accompanied by a dear friend, side by side, sharing reiki with Memes in her final hours. *Full circle moment.* It takes a village, is the truth. My friends continue to cheer me on and see me through the lulls of life. I have a mother who would sacrifice anything for my success and happiness. A father who makes me laugh every time we speak (and is always the first on the dance floor, even if nobody else is). A family that, with all of our differences, finds ways to continue to be inspirational and loving. A very patient man who has never said no to any of my wild ideas or quick shifts in life. Dogs who continue to love me no matter how much I am away from home. I am eternally grateful for each and every person in my life. The journey is good; the community makes it all worthwhile.

Illuminate Purpose
Culmination of purpose. For me, the sadness and feelings of lack because I didn't clearly know what I wanted to be growing up, or my specific purpose for that matter, made me feel like a failure from early on. It was not until I changed the way I looked at purpose that I felt relief. Purpose is not always clear. My overarching purpose in life is to help others, but ask me for details, and you will get many, as you can see in my various stories.

The journey through life includes a culmination of many changes and different purposes at different times, like chapters in the Book of Life. And that's *okay.* Normalizing, not knowing, and trusting the process is important. I am *unboxed*, living my purpose in whatever shape it takes. Just like water, purpose flows; you might as well go with it, rather than against it. Having these touchpoints throughout my life has given me the pillars to form a solid foundation that creates a future filled with purposeful experiences. I now remain present, trust the process, and continuously expand my reach daily.

Illuminate You
There are scenarios that we have all been through that feel overwhelming or scary, but somehow, we manage to navigate them. If you are longing to feel on purpose, decide on the next small attainable step, which will culminate over time into the big picture or the success you are seeking. It is not going to

happen overnight; greatness takes time. It is okay not to be okay, not to know, to be in search of. Believe in yourself and take one step at a time. Don't forget to love all of yourself; it is vital through this process. Most importantly, move toward the moments that illuminate you and light others up.

IGNITE ACTION STEPS

- **Illuminate the unknown.** Sit with it… rest your mind, heart, and soul connection. It is okay not to know. Nothing is set in stone; you have the ability to recreate at any time.

- **Do those things that challenge you.** Don't let things that intimidate you (like public speaking) stop you.

- **Listen in on your gifts,** believe in them, and explore. Let go and flow. Breathe. Believe. Achieve.

Lorena Lee — United States of America
Unboxed Frequency Holder, Facilitator, Activator,
Business Owner, Author, MSW, Reiki Master
www.lorenalee.com
🄾 beingillume

Tina Hatch

TINA HATCH

"You are whole and worthy, a beautiful expression of the Divine."

I wish for you to know in your mind and feel in your heart and soul that you are whole and worthy. You are light and love. You are united with the flow of Divine energy and creation, a unique expression of God. No one can take away your relationship with the Higher Power and Divine Light that guides and resides within you. In your human desire to belong, may you also find the courage to live authentically and know you are held in sacred love with Divine purpose.

YOU ARE DIVINE LIGHT

He lowered me under the water. I came up glowing. I felt holy and light, warm and tingly. I was 8 years old and just baptized into The Church of Jesus Christ of Latter-day Saints (often referred to as LDS or Mormon). I was full of innocent wonder and awe, wrapped in the desire to be as pure and good as possible, following Jesus with all my heart.

I was raised under the blanket of Mormonism that permeated our family and community's culture, beliefs, and worldview. I lived and breathed my family's faith. I'm a 7th-generation Mormon. It runs deep in my veins. I grew up hearing stories of ancestors' faith and dedication retold by family and church members—stories etched in journals long ago and ever present in our collective memory. Growing up, I was confident and loved, grounded in a belief that I was a daughter of God, someone known by a perfect Being who had a purpose for my life. I had a profound sense of my wholeness and spirituality. I was also a silent feminist in the making, a serious people pleaser, and a high achiever wanting approval from those I loved most. I didn't want to let my family or church down. I knew what they expected of me, and I wanted to be *so* good, *so* perfect for them and God. I was part of something larger than myself, and I loved that belonging. I needed it like the intoxicating warmth and safety of a mother's arms around her nursing child. I never imagined that one day that sweet belonging would be painfully at odds with living authentically and speaking my truth.

Growing up in Utah, I was sheltered and naive. Life was seemingly simple and predictable in my very homogenous, very Mormon neighborhood of neatly manicured yards and kind people. My community was full of married, traditional families living according to church teachings. I knew very few people who lived differently and didn't know anyone who was gay. I rarely even heard the word gay or homosexual. One night as a young teenager, I slept over at an aunt's house. She told us about going to a concert and seeing lesbians kiss. She said it was disgusting and horrible. I didn't know what to think, but I was shocked by the level of dislike my aunt felt for gay people. In church, I didn't hear the word gay often, but the message was clear, the only acceptable option was to be straight and married with kids. I learned it was wrong to be 'that way,' someone confused who liked the same sex and did 'unnatural' things. I was taught to 'hate the sin, love the sinner.'

I dated some in high school and college, and had occasional crushes on both men and women. I adored a guy I went to study abroad with in France, but we were never in a relationship. I chalked up my general lackluster interest in men to being more mature than many guys my age and to my growing dislike of patriarchy and sexism that I experienced in my cultural surroundings. I couldn't really see myself ending up with a man in a typical Mormon marriage, but at the same time, it seemed like the only option for a faithful Mormon. Relatives frequently asked me about dating, and some gave me advice on flirting. I knew that wasn't what I needed. I rarely felt attracted emotionally or sexually to men. I had no framework for the possibility that it was an option to like women, and so I completely discounted the crush I had on a girl in high school.

When I turned twenty-one, I went on a mission to Norway for my church. I learned about grace and rejection, love and acceptance. And I learned to trust my own relationship with God. Yet, something else also started to happen. When you go on an LDS mission, you have a peer companion with you at all times. I began feeling a sense of *love and deep attraction* for 2 of my female companions. I wondered how it would be to spend the rest of my life with one of them. It was so beautiful, so pure, so deep. I hadn't felt such an intimate connection to a woman in that way before, and not to a man. *Could I feel this strong emotional bond with a man?* I didn't sexualize the deep connection or define it at the time. I returned home more conflicted about men but determined I would find a way to fall in love and get married. That was my life plan. That was God's intention for me.

I roomed with one of my favorite mission companions in my last year of college. I was jealous when she dated guys. I wanted to be the one dating her. That was my first small inkling that things would be different for me.

Despite the shift beginning to happen, I continued to adhere to my faith tradition. I dated men and had a Mormon boyfriend in graduate school. While I felt a genuine connection and loved him, I broke up with him because I couldn't see myself in a sexual relationship with him. Who I was inside seemed far broader than who I was taught to be and who I felt I could be in a relationship with a man.

In graduate school, one of the staff members was lesbian, the first I had ever met. She was kind and spiritual. She left her position at the end of the year for a new position working for her church. She wasn't a bad person. She was happy. She was good and whole. She didn't match anything I had envisioned from what my church and community had taught me about being gay. And she belonged to a church that accepted her and hired her to do spiritual work, knowing she was lesbian. I was floored, confused, delighted. My world was expanding, and I was coming into a new awareness of myself and new hopefulness for the life I could have. The pieces of the puzzle were starting to come together, and I finally had a framework to understand my sexuality and to allow that understanding to surface. The feelings I was having in high school, and the thoughts I had while on an LDS mission started to make more sense. My attraction toward women was deeper than anything I experienced with men. I felt a longing to explore my sexuality and attraction to women despite what I had been taught.

While in graduate school, I became alive by reading texts on feminism, gender, race, and patriarchy. It was as if the things I had seen and experienced during my life were being articulated in written words in ways that resonated with me on a deep level. As my mind opened up to new

204 / TINA HATCH

possibilities, the glimpse here and there of my attraction to women became a glaring light that I couldn't escape, and thought perhaps I didn't want to. I had a major crush on a woman in my department in graduate school. She was a safe, dreamy crush, someone I could daydream about while still doing everything I was supposed to do in my church. Still, my inner knowing that I was attracted to women was so compelling that I couldn't ignore it. I had a sense of confidence and purpose in what I was feeling. My drive to be honest with myself and true to that inner knowing pressed me forward. I felt limited and confined by the narrow gender and sexuality box of my faith community and very conflicted by what my church had to say about gender norms and 'same-gender attraction.'

I went to counseling and told the first person ever that I was attracted to women. Once I had verbalized it, and owned it, there was no going back. I was both exhilarated and terrified. My worldview was turned upside down. Everything I had been taught about my life purpose no longer made sense. All that I knew and loved, all that I had given my life to, my church, my family—it felt like it was all crumbling before my eyes. The exhilaration of self-awareness was muted by the crushing knowing that taking steps down one path, owning my sexuality and my longing in one area of my life could mean losing belonging and meaningful inclusion in my faith community and bring deep sadness, shame, worry, and judgment from my family and friends.

In the quiet of my room, I furtively searched over fifty years of church talks to find anything positive or redeeming about being gay. None of it was good or affirming. Sexual sin was compared in gravity to murder, and one church leader referenced scripture that it was better to have a millstone hung around your neck than to commit sexual sin. I had been taught that living authentically as a lesbian in a relationship with a woman would lead me to spiritual demise, separation from God and family, and from the Holy Spirit. I felt disbelief, anger, and sadness. I spent hours, days, and months thinking, praying, crying, distraught, confused, and hopeful. I didn't know how I would pull through. I had many vivid dreams, some symbolic and all indicative of the internal conflict I was experiencing between my religious and sexual identities. *Could my life still be rich with purpose and joy if I were true to myself? Could I be a faithful Mormon, serve God, and be gay?*

Life with my Mormon roommates was also a challenge. One of my roommates begged me not to join a lesbian support group when she learned I was questioning my sexuality. She said they would brainwash me into thinking it was okay to be gay. Another roommate moved out, outraged that I had put a sign in our yard against the 2004 proposed marriage amendment in Utah banning gay marriage. She said no good Mormon would support gay people. One night at dinner with my relatives, we got on the topic of LGBTQ issues. My voice quivered, but I spoke up, saying I didn't agree with the Utah marriage amendment or how the church treated gay people. My closest cousin looked at me and said, "Well, maybe they just shouldn't be gay." I left the table shaking. I was so mad and distraught. I cried in the bathroom and left my parents' house without saying goodbye. My cousin asked my brother if I was gay. He said, "You put 2 and 2 together." My cousin chased me, but I hopped in the car and drove away. The whole car ride back to my condo, I sobbed. I pounded the steering wheel. I yelled to God, "Why? Why me? It isn't fair. It just isn't fair. I don't deserve this. I haven't done anything wrong. Make it right. Please. You know my heart." I wanted desperately to be able to be free, to be myself, and be loved for who I was. Yet, I felt the weight of years of church doctrine and cultural bias stacked against me. Part of me wanted everything to go back to normal, back to who I was before Pandora's box had been opened. But part of me knew I couldn't. I wouldn't.

I came to a point where going to church every week was too painful. My faith community was the place I loved most and wanted to belong to, and it was the one place that seemingly did not love me back or want me as I was. It only wanted the image of the woman I had been *told* I should be—married in the temple to a good Mormon man, with kids, making my parents and grandparents proud of me, following the tradition of my faithful pioneer ancestors who had sacrificed so much for me.

After graduate school, I came out quickly at work and in safe social circles, wearing a "bisexuals exist" pin and rainbow flag some days to work. I attended an LGBTQ support group on campus and joined an LGBTQ Mormon Fellowship listserv for affirmation and support. But at church and with most of my family and extended family, it was different, slow, suffocating, painful, and raw. There was little place for me in Mormon theology, and by extension, it felt, in my very Mormon family and community. No matter how good I was or how much I wanted an equal seat at the table, I didn't belong. I was expendable to the institution and faith community I had loved. I felt rejected and unseen.

The next few years were full of dichotomy. It was a period of deep growth, expansion, pain, and loss. I met and fell in love with my future wife, Madeline. She was smart, spiritual, funny, and kind, with a beautiful smile, a soothing voice, and gorgeous curves. Our dating and falling in love years were filled

206 / Tina Hatch

with all the feverish attraction of young love, punctuated by extreme grief that our relationship was not understood or accepted by my church. I experienced complete joy and light with Madeline. I felt giddy, alive, and whole with her and couldn't make sense of the huge gap between what I felt and what I knew my church believed. All that I knew and believed about my goodness and my spiritual connection to God still felt true, and yet suddenly, I felt like an outsider. I knew I was a "sinner" in my faith community's eyes, one who would be excluded from meaningful participation in the space that had fed my spiritual soul for so many years.

I didn't believe what my church and community said about LGBTQ people. Still, part of me was swallowed up with doubt, worry, and fear. The years of profound conditioning in an all-or-nothing theological worldview made it feel almost insurmountable to release the fear that I might be wrong and to make sense of what it meant if I was actually right. *What if all I had believed in and given my life to was not the One truth, the one path for me to follow? What if the LDS church wasn't the only path that could bring me real joy and deep connection with God? What if they were flat-out wrong about LGBTQ people, just like they had been about other racial minorities in their earlier years?* Maybe I could create change from within. Institutions take time to change, but surely they would one day fully include LGBTQ people. *How could my church hold the One path to eternal life with God and my family if there was no room in it for the beautiful love I felt for Madeline? How could I feel so in flow with the Divine in so many moments of deep connection and love with Madeline if it was truly sinful and against God's will to love a woman?* But what if the internal whisperings of my soul were misguided and I was wrong?

During that turbulent time of inner questions and coming out about my sexuality, I had a profound IGNITE moment, one that provided me with deep clarity and peace, and confirmation that my Purpose was broader than the checklist I had been taught at church. I was in the LDS temple, a place that, for Mormons and me at the time, was the most holy place on earth. It was where I would go for inspiration and guidance. I knew I would not be permitted to continue going to the temple since I was dating Madeline. (The temple requires a biennial interview and approval from your church leader to attend.) When I entered the temple that day, my mind was still swirling with deep-down fears. *Would God see through me? Would the temple workers sense I was lesbian and ask me to leave? Was I really okay? Or was I fooling myself? Was it horribly deceitful of me to even go to the temple even though I felt worthy to be there?*

I was dressed in white, sitting in the temple's Celestial room. As I was meditating and praying, a rush of emotion came over me. I felt complete peace, calm, and love. I looked up, and I could see God looking down at me, smiling. Streams of golden light and goodness were pouring down. My whole body felt tingly and warm. I knew this feeling well, and I was relieved to be feeling this way in the temple. I had an out-of-body experience where I could see a very clear image of my future self, with God's love beaming down, and my partner Madeline standing with her arm around me. I was holding a baby girl, and we were together in the Celestial room. I had the clear impression that God didn't just love me; God loved me in a relationship with Madeline and would bless us with our own family. We were whole and good. I knew that day when I walked out of the temple that I was worthy to be there. The church theology and community weren't ready to accept this truth or to see my wholeness. But God already had. The Divine light was already bursting in me and through me whether I was lesbian or not.

I learned during this raw period that God was not cutting me off. God and Christ still knew and loved me. My IGNITE moment in the temple confirmed that I was part of the great stream of God's creation, light, and love, whole and beyond any one limiting identity. My partner and I were also the expressions of the Divine and divine love, in the fullness of who we were: body, flesh, spirit, soul, in our longing and loving of each other and God. I could live with integrity and authenticity and still be blessed by God. I, too, was holy, light, love, with Purpose and worth. The church could misunderstand or even disown me. But they didn't own my spirituality, my faith, and the inner light guiding me. I felt a sense of relief and an opening for courage to move forward on a path of expansion, authenticity, and greater Purpose.

For years after my experience in the temple, despite knowing my wholeness, despite being fully out at work and in my community in a very liberal midwest town, I lived mostly closeted in my faith community, fearing excommunication. I knew it was a matter of luck with Mormon bishops, some very understanding and others towing the church line. 6 years after my experience in the temple, a bishop at church pulled me aside. He asked me why I didn't come to church regularly. I was a returned missionary and had served in the church. I decided it was my moment to be truthful. Scared but tired of working so hard to protect myself, I told him I was gay and happily married to a woman and felt unsafe to be out in the church. The conversation went surprisingly well. He asked to meet again. Unfortunately, our second meeting did not go well. It became a 2-hour interrogation. He threatened church discipline or excommunication if I did not break up with my wife. I left the meeting drained and disappointed but still believing the whisperings of my soul that I was good. I was newly pregnant with our first child and wrapped myself in the wonder and excitement of the growing baby inside of me, delighted every time she kicked and turned.

Over the following months, despite waves of panic and fear about possible excommunication, I leaned into the voice inside of me, the same Divine light that had assured me I was whole in the temple. It would be alright. God was with me. Divine light flowed in me. My inner strength and sense of wholeness and purpose grew. I knew that the covenants I made with God at baptism and in the temple were promises between me and God, not an institution. It gave me a sense of power in my relationship with my church and a greater sense of belonging to myself and God.

Soon after, I gave birth to our beautiful daughter whose name rightfully means 'whole and complete,' 'My God has answered.' She was born in the water. When I brought her up out of the water, she looked at me with deep, wise eyes. The moment was brief but felt eternal. I felt as though I was also reborn, courageous, and whole in the process of bringing our daughter into the world. I was delighted to be a mom and felt so much gratitude for this gift in my life. I would take my daughter to the grocery store when she was a baby and find myself stopped in the aisle, with her cooing at me and me entranced, looking into her deep blue eyes, cooing back at her, and feeling alive and full of purpose and delight. I was a mom. I had a family. Life was good, despite the ups and downs in my faith journey.

In my professional life at the University of Wisconsin-Madison, I was passionate about helping international students. I held a unique international student advisor role with a joint appointment with the Gender and Sexuality Campus Center. As part of my role as advisor and assistant director, I developed online resources for LGBTQ international students. I put on several LGBTQ international events a year to support our students. I helped plan and implement a few LGBTQ student leadership retreats. I loved providing a safe, welcoming space for the students. And while I was still navigating my own journey toward greater authenticity within my faith community and sexuality, I felt a real purpose in listening and holding space for international and LGBTQ students to be seen and honored on their own journeys.

3 years after our daughter was born, our son came into the world. I was beside myself, happy to have another child. Our dear friend, Dory, had blessed our daughter when she was a baby. A good, strong, woman's voice blessing our

daughter in the most beautiful way I could ask for. This time, I thought I was strong enough in my complicated faith journey to ask my dad to bless our son. It is a formal LDS ritual performed by a male priesthood holder, but one we could do at my house in a safe, sacred space. I was working up the courage to ask my dad when the LDS church announced in 2015 their exclusion policy that the children of gay parents could not be blessed or baptized into the LDS church and that married gay couples were apostates subject to church discipline. Despite the heartache and anger I felt, I also felt a growing surge of confidence inside of me, calling me to walk authentically in all parts of my life, knowing I wanted my children to be able to do the same.

I met with a new bishop at that time. "What do you want," he asked. I told him I wanted to be able to bring all of me to church and be able to serve. "That's asking too much," he said. He knew my heart was good but asked me to continue to show up quietly closeted. Then he told me, "I'm sorry. I don't see anything in church for your family." Despite tears running down my face, I left our meeting awakened, and changed, the light inside me burning bright. At that moment, the heavens opened, and a shift happened inside of me that I needed to start healing more profoundly. It was a gift. Another IGNITE moment propelling me toward greater Purpose and courage. It allowed me to see with clarity that I couldn't live my entire life trying to belong in a space that didn't see my wholeness, no matter how much I longed to be seen and held in that space. I realized I needed to let go and expand. I could not be spiritually whole whilst living in fear. I could not be authentically me if I continued to co-sign to spaces that asked me to hide. I came to know my greater Purpose was to live authentically in wholeness, light, and joy, openly honoring both my sexuality and spirituality and holding sacred space for others to do the same, recognizing the Divine that flows within us all. I belonged to the great I AM, connected to those who saw themselves as separate from me. I belonged because I am. I belonged because I breathe. I was beautifully Mormon, lesbian, a mom, broken and whole, part of the One. I was perfectly human and alive, writing my own story.

I began worshiping with my wife and kids in LGBTQ-affirming spaces. I allowed myself space to soak in God's love expressed in new sacred places, in nature, in community with others, and in my heart. I let myself come more fully home, recognizing in my yearning to belong that I had always belonged to God, to myself, and to the great stream of light and love uniting us all. I felt a deep connection and love in new faith communities with people who affirmed what I had known for so long, that I am whole, I am loved, and my marriage is just as available for God's presence and light as anyone else's. My LGBTQ identity is an equally beautiful and Divine part of me, as is my deep spirituality, curiosity, laughter, empathy, and love to connect across cultures. My love for my wife is not a broken or sinful part of me. My wounds and heartache came not from loving her but from being seen as separate, sinful, and broken by those around me.

In allowing this expansion of consciousness, I feel deeper self-compassion, more able to love myself and others and live out my greater Purpose in wholeness and integrity. I can breathe deeper and more consistently honor the Divine light inside of me. I don't have to give up the parts of my faith tradition that I still love. But I don't have to cling to my longing to belong either or continue to allow spiritual harm in order to hold my ground, speak my truth, and claim the Divine within me. I finally let go, surrendered, and let in. I am free. I am Divine light and love.

You are also light and love. No matter what others say or believe about you, no matter what identities people place on you or that you hold close to your heart, you are part of something larger, beyond your ego, part of the great stream of light and love uniting us all. You belong. You have the Divine within you and are worthy and whole. When you fear rejection for speaking your truth and being your higher self, know that the world needs you and your voice, your unique imprint. When you feel the deep tug between belonging and the desire to live authentically, may you be gentle with yourself and trust your inner voice as your path unfolds. When the need for authenticity and integrity to yourself is so deep that it calls you forward to speak and live your truth no matter the cost, have courage and know you will be held and seen. You are not alone. We are each called into greater belonging with the Divine, coming home to ourselves, honoring our wholeness, healing our wounds, and living in deep Purpose and authenticity. The journey is a dance, one worth doing over and over again. I am dancing with you, seeing your beauty, and holding you in a sacred space. May you have the courage to live aligned with your purpose and shine the light that radiates intensely inside of you.

IGNITE ACTION STEPS

- **Listen to your inner voice and follow the light inside you.** Trust your intuition and the inspired thoughts that come to you when you are still and quiet. Write down inspired thoughts and experiences to remember in difficult times.

- **Speak your truth and find ways to live authentically.** Practice finding twenty seconds of courage daily to speak and live your truth.

- **Find spiritual practices and daily rituals that help you experience wholeness and joy.** Meditate, pray, be in nature, dance, breathe, and listen. You are wise and capable of following the right path for your growth and expansion.

- **Connect with God/your Higher Power, and remember that no one owns your spirituality or inner truth.** Hold your hand on your heart, take a deep breath, and imagine warm golden light encompassing, healing, and holding you. You have the Divine within you, and at your essence are light and love.

Tina Hatch — United States of America
Advisor and Spiritual Coach, Author, Speaker, Healing Work, International
Educator, Entrepreneur, LGBTQ Advocate, Women Empowerment
tinahatch2000@gmail.com
⬛ Tina Hatch
⬛ tina.hatch1
⬛ tina-hatch-792067138

Peter Giesin

PETER GIESIN

"Your potential is a God-given gift."

In the delicate balance of life's highs and lows, I call on you to embrace your destiny, understanding that in the vast tapestry of existence, every moment has its purpose. With courage, choose to navigate the profound journey of discovery, not just across the expanse of time but deep within your own soul, realizing the boundless potential of the human spirit.

WHISPERS OF DESTINY

I had it all, or at least, that's what it looked like from the outside. The term "American Dream" wasn't just a phrase to me; it was a living reality. With a supporting wife, 2 vibrant children, and a dog that bounded around our home with infectious energy, our domestic life was a tapestry of cherished moments. Our evenings were often comprised of laughter, with stories shared over dinner, spontaneous dance sessions in our living room, and walks in the nearby park, with our playful pooch darting around, trying to chase the evening butterflies. The love and warmth in our household were palpable, a haven I would retreat to after my business escapades.

But the world outside our loving home was vastly different, challenging, and demanding. My profession as a tech prodigy meant I wasn't just confined to the towering glass buildings of New York City—I was a global entity, traveling across continents, navigating time zones, and immersing myself in diverse cultures. My name was known in tech hubs from San Francisco to New York City, and beyond. Boardrooms buzzed with anticipation when I walked in, ready to impart guidance on the next big software platform. When the discussions got heated, the serene memories of my family would be the calming anchor that kept me grounded.

Yet, despite the roaring applause and hefty paychecks, a part of me felt like an actor on a world stage, playing a part with practiced ease, while my inner self yearned for those simple moments—like reading bedtime stories to my kids or enjoying a quiet morning run through the neighborhood.

During one of my many international ventures, fate intervened, pulling me out of that existential crisis, but at a hefty emotional price. Frankfurt, with its blend of modernity and medieval charm, was a city I'd grown to appreciate. Its historical architecture juxtaposed against the futuristic sky-line was a reflection of my life—rooted in traditions yet flying high on the wings of technology. The process was cut short as I expertly worked through another successful project. The sharp pain, starting as a dull ache, quickly amplified, gripping my chest with an intensity I had never experienced. I felt a weight pressing down on me as if trying to ground me, tying me down to the very roots I'd been soaring above. Moments, memories, regrets, and dreams all flashed before my eyes in that split second, plunging me into an all-encompassing darkness. The next thing I knew, the world around me had shifted drastically.

The world I awakened to was surprisingly tranquil. A cozy café, seemingly plucked straight from an old-world painting, beckoned me. The intricacies of its wooden interiors reflected years of craftsmanship, each grain telling a tale. Amber light emanated from vintage bulbs overhead, casting elongated shadows that danced with every flicker. Every so often, the gentle ring of the doorbell would announce a new patron, but the conversations were but a soft hum in the background.

I felt oddly at peace, wrapped in the comforting scents that filled the air. The delicate scent of freshly baked pretzels wafted through, each wave inter-mingling with the rich aroma of brewing coffee. It was a paradoxical scene, a space where time seemed to stand still while the world outside continued its relentless pace.

As I tried to make sense of this surreal environment, my attention was drawn to a man seated across from me. It wasn't just his familiar eyes or the lines that mapped his face; it was an innate recognition, a soul-deep understanding that this was a reflection of me from another time, perhaps another life. His introduction as Avram wasn't as startling as his message. The possibility of destiny, the challenges of longevity, and the beauty of existence were wrapped in his every word.

The air grew still as Avram leaned in, his gaze locking onto mine, and in a tone that seemed to resonate from the depths of time itself, he delivered his prophecy:

"Once, flying was a dream until the Wright Brothers dared to soar. Similarly, living beyond age's known bounds awaits its pioneer. Peter, you're poised to be that trailblazer. Stand firm in faith and self-belief. But remember, with such longevity comes a unique solitude, as you'll outlive both loved ones and the generation that follows. Your path may be solitary, but it's profound."

Every word struck me like a chord, vibrating through my very essence. Not merely because of the profound nature of the prophecy but because of the recognition that this was about me, about my destiny. The weight of his words, their implications, and the vast stretch of time he spoke of were overwhelming. It felt as though the ground beneath me had shifted, and I was standing on the edge of an uncharted frontier.

Jerking back to reality in a sterile hospital room was disorienting. The white ceiling tiles stared down at me, punctuated by blinding fluorescent lights. The rhythmic beeping of heart monitors and the faint whispers of hurried medical jargon surrounded me. Tubes and wires tethered me to various machines, reminding me of my vulnerability. Each inhale tasted sterile, the antiseptic aroma a sharp contrast to the warmth of the café I'd just left.

As I began to regain consciousness in the white surroundings of the hospital room, my mind was a blur, trying to piece together the fragments of memories that led me to this moment. The room felt oddly calm, a stark contrast to the chaos I could faintly recall before everything went dark.

In the dim light filtering in, I noticed a figure approaching me. It was Dr. Abraham, the attending physician. He had an air of solemnity about him, but his eyes were kind and understanding. Pulling up a chair beside my bed, he took a deep breath and began to speak with a gentle yet earnest tone.

"You gave us quite a scare," he began, his voice slightly trembling. "For nearly 5 minutes your heart stopped beating, we lost you. You were... gone. Dead, to put it bluntly."

A cold shiver ran down my spine as the weight of his words settled in. I could see the toll the experience had taken on him as well, the lines of exhaustion and worry evident on his face. But there was something else in his eyes, a glimmer of awe or perhaps respect.

"It's nothing short of a miracle that you're here now, talking to me," he continued. "The human spirit is truly astounding. Your will to live, your potential, it's truly a gift, not a burden."

The realization of how close I had come to the end and the gravity of the situation left me overwhelmed. But in that vulnerability, there was also a newfound clarity and appreciation for life and its mysterious ways.

As shocking as that vision was, the words from the ancient gentleman echoed in the depths of my mind. The profound implications of our conversation lingered, creating a tumult of emotions. Fear, skepticism, curiosity, and an undeniable weight of responsibility bore down on me. *Would this vision redefine my existence? Or was it simply a manifestation of my subconscious, a dream amplified by my physical state?* The profound gravity of Avram's prophecy, coupled with the immediate concern for my health and my family, created an emotional dichotomy that was overwhelming. It felt like I stood on the precipice of a revelation, with one foot in a realm of mystic possibilities and the other firmly rooted in the tangible present.

Following that episode, my life shifted internally in ways I couldn't have anticipated. Every interaction, every emotion, and every decision was now tinged with an undercurrent of uncertainty and dread. I'd always considered myself to be a rational individual. My success in the tech world was built upon logic, methodical thinking, and clear-cut decisions. Yet, here I was, grappling with a mystical vision that seemed anything but logical.

Night after night, I'd lie awake, staring into the abyss of my ceiling as my mind raced in loops. Every chuckle of my child, every intimate moment with my wife, and even the simple joy of a family meal took on heightened significance. *Were these the moments I'd cherish when I was living in a world where they no longer existed?* The specter of outliving everyone I cherished was haunting, to say the least.

It wasn't just about my potential longevity; it was the profound loneliness that Avram had forewarned. The sheer thought of witnessing generations pass, being the last one standing amongst my contemporaries, was more chilling than any concept of mortality. At gatherings, as laughter echoed and memories were made, a tiny part of me would involuntarily drift into the realm of 'what ifs.' *What if these very friends aged, withered, and left while I remained a relic of a time gone by?*

Despite this turmoil within, I maintained a façade of normalcy. I didn't want to burden my loved ones with these abstract fears. The vulnerability of that hospital room was still fresh, and sharing my vision might amplify their concerns for my mental well-being. What's more, how could I articulate a vision so fantastical, so implausible, without sounding unhinged? It felt like a secret too vast, too overwhelming to share. I wrestled with the idea of saddening my family with the burden of my potential longevity and the solitude that might come with it. Fearing the chasm of understanding it could create or the pitiful glances that might follow, I chose silence.

I buried my story and fears deep, trying to cloak them behind a renewed zest for life. I threw myself into work, into the family, into hobbies. Maybe if I stayed busy enough, I mused, the fears would diminish. However, despite my efforts, there was always a moment, often in the quiet of the night or during a solitary walk, when Avram's words would resurface, casting their long, inescapable shadow.

Yet, as time passed, life had its way of embedding distractions. The rhythmic routine of day-to-day existence—meetings, school events, weekend outings, and holidays—worked like a balm, momentarily easing my inner turmoil. My child's milestones, our family trips, the warmth of our home during festivities, all these experiences seemed to wrap me in a protective cocoon. The simple joy of watching our dog chase after a ball in the park or the pleasure of a lazy Sunday morning with my kids provided moments of genuine happiness. And in those moments, Avram's daunting prophecy faded to the background, if only for a fleeting while.

Of course, the Universe has a peculiar way of nudging us. Every so often, an event would jolt me back to that conversation in the café. It could be something as benign as a film about immortality, a book discussing the human lifespan, or a chance conversation with a stranger about the mysteries of existence. These were seemingly unrelated incidents, yet for me, they were poignant reminders of the path I was possibly destined for.

One such profound incident occurred at an art exhibition. Among the myriad of colors and strokes, there stood a magnificent rendition of Leonardo Da Vinci's Vitruvian Man. I was inexplicably drawn to it, the perfection of the human form depicted with mathematical precision. It was a celebration of human potential and capability. Looking at it, I felt an overwhelming urge to ink it onto my skin, a permanent reminder of the boundless possibilities within us and perhaps a subtle nod to my encounter with Avram. The very act of getting that tattoo felt like a surrender, an acknowledgment of the extraordinary journey that might lie ahead.

As with all things, the initial rush of such an acknowledgment faded, and life resumed its course. The tattoo became a part of me, often forgotten under layers of clothing, much like the vision buried under layers of denial. In the company of loved ones, it was easier to immerse myself in the moment, letting the distant worries of tomorrow stay shrouded in the mists of time.

Amid the intricate dance of destiny, my heart stumbled upon an unfamiliar beat. My marriage, which once flourished under dawn's optimistic glow, found itself enveloped in twilight's mournful shade. Fifteen years, filled with shared dreams, whispered secrets, and tender moments, began to fray at the edges, tainted by the cold touch of betrayal. The pain was acute, piercing every corner of my soul, etching scars that spoke louder than words about trust shattered and love betrayed.

There were nights when the weight of it all threatened to crush me, where the echoes of my past reverberated through the silent walls, and the bed felt too vast and empty. The ghost of her laughter, the memory of shared plans, and the haunting emptiness of lost potential consumed me.

But in the silent recesses of my heart, a contradictory emotion emerged—relief. It seemed almost blasphemous to feel it amidst the storm of emotions, yet there it was. The somber realization that the inevitable weight of outliving her, of enduring decades of seeing the love of my life age while I remained unchanging, was a burden I no longer had to bear. This paradoxical liberation was both my solace and my torment.

While the threads of grief, relief, and a yearning for closure twisted together, the horizon hinted at a new dawn. And even amidst the heartache, the journey whispered promises, reminding me that after the darkest night, there's always a new day waiting to be embraced.

The tapestry of my life, filled with its unpredictable turns, unraveled a luminous strand 7 years later. As the scars from my past began their slow fade, the Universe, in all its vast, mysterious kindness, led me to her—a beacon of spiritual profundity, an ethereal vision of joy and wisdom. Her presence emanated an energy so palpable that even those blind to spiritual vibrations felt drawn to her. Her laughter, it was the kind that could chase away the darkest clouds, and her very being infused me with a tranquility I'd thought was forever lost.

Our paths didn't cross by mere chance. It felt preordained, as though the cosmos, whispering winds, and destiny itself had schemed in perfect harmony to intertwine our stories. Yet, I remained guarded. Memories of Avram's prophecy cast a long, chilling shadow, urging me to protect myself, to keep her at a distance. I cherished our moments together but always with a shielded heart, fearing the expanse of time that might one day tear us apart. I had told her, time and time again, that while I valued our bond immensely, it could only be that of deep friendship. Marriage, I believed, was a door I had firmly shut.

Yet the Universe, in its infinite wisdom, wasn't done with me. During a shared journey to Antelope Canyon, surrounded by time-sculpted red rocks echoing millennia of stories, something within me began to stir. The canyon, with its whispers of eons gone by, seemed to resonate with that silent, guarded part of my soul. As if the ancient stones themselves throbbed with a message, urging me to see, feel, and embrace the love that stood right before me.

In that awe-inspiring embrace of nature, amidst the fiery embrace of the canyon walls and the ethereal play of light, emotions welled up, overpowering every defense I'd set up. Those walls I'd built crumbled, and the weight of the prophecy felt distant, less binding. With the vast, timeless canyon as my witness, I found myself kneeling, drawn by a force beyond my comprehension. I professed my deep, unwavering devotion to this incredible woman before me. The echoes of the canyon stood as a testament to a love that promised to defy time and every foretold destiny.

In the early glow of our marriage, countless nights were spent sharing stories, dreams, and unspoken fears. The intimacy that blossomed between us was profound, each moment feeling like we were peeling away layers, getting to the very core of our beings. One such night, as the soft luminescence of the moon spilled through our window, she turned to me, her eyes, those deep wells of emotion, shimmering with a mixture of serenity and sadness.

Drawing a deep breath, she whispered, "I've had a vision." Her voice quivered, not with fear, but with a raw vulnerability that immediately arrested my attention. "I see myself at one hundred," she continued, "It's peaceful, calm. I'm lying there, and you're holding me, your warmth enveloping me. As my last breath leaves me, I'm in your arms. That's how I wish to depart from this world."

The room grew silent, the weight of her words pressing down on us. The very essence of the moment seemed to freeze. I could feel the rhythm of our heartbeats, once in sync, now resonating with different emotions.

Her revelation shattered the fragile peace that I'd been nurturing within myself. It was like a violent storm sweeping through a serene landscape, uprooting everything in its path. The walls of that inner cage I'd been painstakingly dismantling brick by brick suddenly seemed to rebuild themselves, higher and more formidable than before.

The cruel irony of my destiny hit me anew. The prophecy, which I had been trying to reconcile with, resurfaced with a vengeance, reminding me of the heart-wrenching fate that awaited. A life beyond the bounds of normal human existence, a life where I'd witness the ebb of time claiming all my loved ones. The fabric of our shared reality, the dreams we were weaving together, felt like they were being torn apart, thread by thread.

The vision she shared, intended as a tender moment of raw honesty, had inadvertently sent me spiraling back into the confines of my fears. The juxtaposition of her serene acceptance of mortality against my eternal timeline was a harsh reminder of the chasm that existed between our destinies.

My fifty-fifth birthday began like any other. It was a day filled with the warmth of well-wishes, the sound of laughter, and the delightful surprises that age hadn't yet managed to steal the joy from. Yet, as the sun dipped below the horizon, casting golden hues across the sky, a familiar unease crept in. The evening, which began as a celebration, soon took on a tone of introspection as the hours waned.

It was during these twilight moments, amid quiet reflection, that he reappeared. Avram, now seemingly even older but retaining that uncanny resemblance to me, was sitting in the living room where my family had gathered earlier. The space, which had echoed with jubilation, was now wrapped in a hush, the weight of our previous encounter palpable.

"Time has passed, hasn't it?" Avram began, his voice a gentle, weathered whisper. "And yet, while you've aged, your journey's purpose seems buried, almost forgotten."

I looked at him, the manifestation of my fate, a mirror into a potential future. His eyes held centuries of stories, of love found and lost, adventures taken and avoided, and moments cherished and regretted. Every wrinkle, every gray hair, seemed to speak of a lifetime of experiences.

"We meet again, not as a mere reminder," he continued, "But as a beckoning to embrace your destiny. Your struggles and your avoidance haven't gone unnoticed. But remember, your potential isn't a curse, but a gift."

I swallowed hard, the weight of my years and my journey pressing down. "Why now?" I managed to ask, my voice barely above a whisper.

"Because," Avram responded, his gaze unwavering, "Your heart has always known the truth, even when your mind tried to reject it. The Universe is persistent. It will keep knocking until its message is heeded."

He leaned forward, bridging the distance between us, and added, "Living a life in fear of your destiny is no life at all. It's time you face it, embrace it, and let yourself truly live. Only then will you realize that, in the end, you won't be as alone as you fear."

The room seemed to expand and contract with his words, every molecule charged with meaning. In that instant, I felt the decades ahead and the decades behind. I stood, once again, at the crossroads of belief and skepticism, but this time, with a clearer understanding of the journey I might undertake.

Then, just as the morning sun began to pierce the horizon with its first rays, there was a shift. An almost imperceptible change in the atmosphere that felt both strange and familiar. As I sat there, rooted to my spot, memories from my life played before my eyes. Each event, each emotion, was amplified, resonating deeply within me. They weren't just my memories anymore; they felt universal, as though they belonged to every person who'd ever lived.

I remembered the innocent joy of my childhood, playing without a care in the world. The turbulent years of adolescence filled with confusion and the desperate need to fit in. The pride and weight of responsibility that came with becoming a parent. The quiet moments with my wife, where no words were needed, and our souls seemed to communicate on their own. And then, there were the times of loneliness, doubt, and fear. These memories seemed to echo Avram's long life and served as a stark reminder of our shared human experience.

"You see," Avram began, his voice pulling me back from the depths of my reverie, "Life is a tapestry of moments. Some are bright filled with joy and love, while others are shaded with pain and loss. But every thread, no matter its hue, adds to the beauty of the whole. Your journey, should you choose to embrace it, will be no different. Yes, there will be challenges and moments of despair, but there will also be unparalleled beauty, love, and discovery."

I looked into his age-old eyes, searching for answers. "But the thought of outliving everyone... the isolation..." My voice trailed off, the weight of that future pressing down on me.

Avram nodded in understanding. "It's a valid fear," he acknowledged. "But remember, time is a relative concept. As you grow, evolve, and transcend, your perception of time will also change. Relationships, connections, they won't be bound by the traditional constructs you know now. New friendships will form, new bonds will be made. The world will change, and so will you. The essence of who you are will remain, but the way you interact with the world and its inhabitants will evolve."

He leaned in closer, ensuring I caught every word. "Your destiny isn't just about longevity; it's about depth, growth, and understanding. It's about shattering preconceived notions and setting a new standard for human potential. By living your truth, you'll inspire, you'll lead, and most importantly, *you'll never truly be alone.*"

A heavy silence filled the room, punctuated only by the rhythmic ticking of the clock. I sat there, absorbing Avram's words, feeling both daunted and inspired. My life, my path, felt larger than I'd ever imagined, and in that moment, the fear of isolation seemed a small price to pay for such a profound journey.

As dawn painted the sky in hues of orange and gold, a profound sense of clarity washed over me. Avram's words, while daunting, echoed with a truth that resonated deep within my soul. The world outside began to stir, but in that room, time seemed suspended, allowing me to introspect and grapple with the vastness of the destiny before me.

In the delicate balance between day and night, a metaphor for my life began to unfold. Just as the day promises the warmth of the sun but eventually gives way to the cool embrace of night, so too does life oscillate between moments of joy and sorrow. But isn't it the very dance of light and shadow that paints the most beautiful of sunrises and sunsets? Isn't it the interplay of highs and lows that give life its depth and meaning?

From the window, a single ray of sunlight pierced through, casting a golden path across the floor. It was as if nature itself was signaling a new beginning, a path illuminated with promise and potential. With every heartbeat, I could feel the pull of destiny, the magnetic force drawing me toward a journey of unparalleled discovery.

The whispers of the trees, the songs of the birds, and the very pulse of the earth seemed to resonate with Avram's message. I was not just a passive spectator in this vast theatre of existence; I had a role to play, a narrative to weave. The Universe, in all its infinite wisdom, had chosen me to be a beacon of possibility, a testament to the boundless potential of the human spirit.

And so, with a heart brimming with courage and a spirit touched by destiny, I decided to embrace my path. For in the vast tapestry of life, every thread, no matter how seemingly insignificant, has its purpose. And, as the world around me came alive with the promise of a new day, I realized that perhaps the most profound journeys are not those that take us farthest from home, but those that lead us deepest within ourselves.

In that ethereal moment of dawn, a verse formed in my mind, encapsulating the essence of my revelation:

Whispers of Destiny

In the dance of dawn and twilight's song,
Through life's highs and shadows long,
Every soul has its tale to tell,
A destiny where dreams do dwell.
For in the heart of time's vast sea,
Lies the truth of what one can be.
Embrace the journey, face the unknown,
For in doing so, one's purpose is shown.

With these profound words resonating deep within me, a flood of peace washes over my being, a sensation I've never felt with such intensity before. The vast expanse of the future, with its unpredictable twists and turns, looms ahead, holding promises of trials, tribulations, and moments of doubt. The landscape of tomorrow is shrouded in the mists of uncertainty, and yet, there's an underlying clarity piercing through the fog. It's not just about foreseeing what's to come but a profound realization about my own resilience, adaptability, and the innate human spirit to rise above adversities. It's an awakening, a call to a journey not just of external exploration but of inner discovery. Every past experience and every lesson learned has prepared me for *this very moment*. And while the path ahead might be strewn with obstacles, my spirit feels invigorated, determined, and undeterred. There's an undeniable truth staring back at me: I am poised, ready, and eager to embark on the most transformative odyssey of my existence, to truly discover what it means to live, love, and leave a lasting legacy.

As the wisdom of my story unfolds before you, it is my deepest desire that each word, each emotion, finds a mirror in the corridors of your own heart, urging you toward greater clarity and passion. May the essence of my journey blend seamlessly with the rhythms of your own aspirations, serving not just as a distant tale but as a lighthouse guiding you through the vast sea of life's uncertainties. I've danced with destiny, and embraced the unknown, and now I hand over to you the distilled lessons from the voyage of my heart and soul. Let these not merely be words on a page but a compass pointing you toward your true North. Here, I share with you 5 pearls of wisdom, each one forged in the crucible of experience, meant to inspire, guide, and illuminate your own path as you embark on the most profound odyssey of your lifetime.

Ignite Action Steps

1. **Seek Wisdom from Ancient Texts**
   Find a serene corner where the energies feel just right in your living space. Devote time daily to immerse yourself in ancient texts, philosophies, or writings that resonate with your spirit. These age-old teachings often carry truths that remain relevant, serving as a compass as you navigate the path to your destiny.

2. **Cultivate Diverse Relationships**
   Broaden your social circles to include individuals from varied age groups and backgrounds. Whether it's a youthful enthusiast's group or a gathering of experienced elders, these interactions will enrich your life. By building connections based on shared values and dreams, you'll find support and camaraderie that can help counter the feelings of isolation or being 'out of sync' with your generation.

3. **Chronicle Your Journey**
   Consider maintaining a journal or diary where you can introspectively detail your daily experiences. This isn't just a tool for self-reflection but could serve as a legacy. Your writings can act as guideposts for others on a similar journey or simply as a testament to a life lived with purpose.

4. **Prioritize Continuous Learning**
   Never let the fire of curiosity wane. Dedicate time to explore, learn, and evolve. This could mean enrolling in classes, traveling to unfamiliar destinations, or simply attending lectures and seminars. To truly embrace your purpose, it's essential to consistently grow in both wisdom and experience.

5. **Organize Thought-Provoking Gatherings**
Host periodic gatherings where like-minded individuals can engage in deep, meaningful conversations. These could be in your backyard under the stars or any place that feels conducive to open dialogue. Topics can range from destiny, philosophy, to the very essence of human existence. Such interactions not only challenge your perspectives but also reinforce your connection to the greater universe and your overarching purpose.

Embracing one's destiny is no small feat. Still, with these recommendations inspired by my story, I hope you discover actionable steps to move closer to your purpose and live a life intertwined with depth, enjoyment, reverence, and peace.

Peter Giesin — Canada
CoFounder & CTO at Ignite Publishing,
Longevity Coach, Author, Adventurer
peter@igniteyou.life

Purpose Prompt 10

MY PURPOSE INVOLVING MY IGNITE MOMENT

Review your life and find the moment that had a massive impact on you and influenced a major decision that changed the course of your life and sparked a new purpose in you.

_____

_____

_____

_____

_____

_____

_____

_____

_____

_____

_____

_____

Moving forward with Purpose

As these stories conclude, it marks not the end but just the beginning for you. This is where you shift from spectator to contributor. Now that you have defined your purpose, witnessed its impact, and learned its many facets you are primed to embark upon your own journey of a purpose-driven life. Like the many other authors whose purpose-filled path has led them to something greater, the same is about to unfold for you. Your next chapter is about to be graced with all the many blessings that come with living *in* that truth. Honor such a gift.

As you embody the very purpose you have been given, bask in how you feel. Seep deep into the cornucopia of emotions that bloom forth in the richness of you; being in your purposefullness. A life with purpose is a life filled with igniting hearts.

"Your purpose is your destiny."

—Lady JB Owen

IMPORTANT NOTES

What was my favorite story/stories and why?

_____

_____

_____

_____

_____

What are my top 5 greatest learnings and takeaways?

1. _____

2. _____

3. _____

4. _____

5. _____

What did I learn about myself?

_____

_____

_____

_____

_____

How can I use my purpose to Ignite the lives of others?

_____

_____

_____

_____

_____

_____

_____

_____

_____

_____

What action steps do I need to take?

1. _____

2. _____

3. _____

4. _____

5. _____

IGN▮TE™
your
Purpose

RESOURCES OUR *IGNITE YOUR PURPOSE* AUTHORS RECOMMEND

Kanika Rose Raney
- Empowerment: https://iamremarkable.withgoogle.com/
- Empowerment: Book - The Gifts of Imperfection by Brene' Brown
- Empowerment: Instagram and YouTube - melissadawnsimkins
- Empowerment: Instagram and YouTube - liftingasweclimbconsulting
- Empowerment: Instagram - mysticmama11
- Wellness: https://www.healthyselves.com/
- Wellness: https://chefbeee.com/
- Wellness: https://www.carrykumba.com/
- Career Reinvention: Book - Working Identity by Herminia Ibarra
- Wealth & Financial Freedom: https://www.hallwm.com/https:/
- Wealth & Financial Freedom: https://wealthteainc.com/
- Community for Women Entrepreneurs: /helloseven.co/

Kathy Stubbs
- https://adironndaspiritualhealer.org

Lorena Norman
- Eckhart Tolle "A New Earth"

Loretta M. Mitchell
- https://Menus.kryon.com
- https://stargatecircles.com

Nicole S. Freeman
- https://www.biblegateway.com

Randy Dyck
- Me, Myself, and My Brother

Sharni Quinn
- https://sharniquinn.com/ebook/ - Free eBook - 'Superwoman Unplugged: 5 Simple Steps to Live Your Best Life... By Doing Less!'
- https://sharniquinn.com/masterclass/ - Free Masterclass Video - How to unplug from the daily hustle, realign to your purpose and redesign your life for the better!
- www.sharniquinn.com/subscribe - Join Sharni's list for weekly wellness insights and inspiring free resources.
- https://sharniquinn.com/life-coaching/ - Discover Your Purpose - Book your free 30-minute Coaching call with Sharni.
- https://sharniquinn.com/retreats/ - Join Sharni on a Retreat in Bali.

Tina Hatch
- I am Light, by Indie Arie, https://www.youtube.com/watch?v=Lzm4RBlCCQo
- Oprah's Super Soul Podcast
- Mormon Stories Podcast
- A Thoughtful Faith, Episode 382
- Human Rights Campaign, https://www.hrc.org/resources/faith-resources
- Affirmation, https://affirmation.org/
- Book, The Universal Christ: How a Forgotten Reality Can Change Everything We See, Hope For, and Believe. Richard Rohr
- Sunstone Magazine, https://sunstone.org/

Xila C. Hope
- Americans with Disability Act.
- Go here to see information about how the organization: HIS Wingspan, works with the youth through The Dip Show Project: www.hiswingspan.com/thedipshow
- Individuals with Disabilities Education Act.
- Maternal deaths in the U.S. spiked in 2021, CDC Reports. Retrieved from :https://www.npr.org/sections/health-shots/2023/03/16/1163786037/maternal-deaths-in-the-u-s-spiked-in-2021-cdc-reports
- Maternal Mortality Rates in the United States: https://www.cdc.gov/nchs/data/hestat/maternal-mortality/2021/maternal-mortality-rates-2021.htm
- Maxwell Leadership Bible. Thomas Nelson, Inc. (1 Timothy 4:12, Hosea 4:6, Proverbs 8:1, Habakkuk 2:2)

PROJECT LEADERS

JB OWEN

Lady JB Owen is a fearless female leader, internationally bestselling author, global brand builder, award-winning businesswoman, celebrated humanitarian, coveted speaker, trainer, and legacy mentor.

JB's entrepreneurial spirit and dedication to making a positive impact have led her to combine business with inspiration in an innovative way. Forbes Magazine has dubbed Lady JB the "Heart-Centred Publisher," Entrepreneur Magazine has called her a "Female Entrepreneur Determined to Change the World," and Apple News added her name to their "Top 50 Entrepreneurs to Watch." As founder and CEO of Ignite Publishing™, Lady JB has published over 700 authors from 47 countries. She teaches global business owners how to tell their story in a way that makes them a world-renowned brand. She mentors on legacy and creating lasting impact for generations to come.

KJIRSTEN SIGMUND

Kjirsten is known internationally as a Master Consciousness Teacher and Healer in many lineages who are pursuing true liberation and freedom for all beings in humanity.

A Canadian-born master spiritual teacher and healer who has been teaching for more than 17 years, Kjirsten's healing classes are world-renowned, and her unique teachings include evening talks, weekend intensives, seminar events, silent retreats, live internet broadcasts, and online courses.

Kjirsten teaches transformation to every level of student, from novice to seasoned professional. Her classes are rich in humor, insight, and technical teaching. She is gifted with an ability to help people transcend unconscious limitations and find more inner-peace and joy in their lives. She is the creator of the ground-breaking program "Uncommon Wisdom" which translates ancient wisdom into modern-day teachings for spiritual liberation. This powerful 4-day, unforgettable journey into the depths of yourself is focused on exploring the nature of consciousness and the ancient wisdom practices of the sages who understood how to master the art of meeting life with pure presence, power, and awakened purpose.

Born Kjirsten Sigmund in 1985 in Vancouver, British Columbia, Kjirsten grew up as an athlete and competitive soccer player. At age 21, she experienced a full kundalini awakening and became interested in full enlightenment, began to meditate, and became fully absorbed in a quest for ultimate Truth.

In addition to a degree in Human Kinetics, Kjirsten draws upon her decades of study with a wide range of spiritual teachers, mystics, North and South American shamans, yogis, Tibetan, Buddhist, and yogic masters, and several fully enlightened beings with a focus on meditation, transfiguration, mysticism, shamanism, higher consciousness, metaphysics, quantum physics, neuroscience, and positive psychology.

Conveying key spiritual principles with a distinct clarity and wisdom that enables frequent epiphanies in others, during each interaction with Kjirsten, she creates a sacred space in which she works multi-dimensionally to manifest the greatest transformational change within every student's vast consciousness and psyche.

Inspired by a vision for global liberation, Kjirsten has dedicated her life to serving humanity with absolute grace and the radical presence of unconditional love and detached compassion.

Kjirsten Sigmund is also a dynamic Canadian entrepreneur and the founder and Executive Chair of Vancouver-based higher consciousness consulting agency Uncommon Wisdom Consulting Corporation as well as LIFE Looking Inside For Everything Communications Corp/Global Life Wellness, a marketing hub for higher consciousness service providers to offer their services to the world for greater levels of healing and growth. So far, these companies have manifested millions of dollars in sales and are growing rapidly.

After launching UWCC, it has grown steadily, servicing a wide demographic of individuals and organizations. Unlike most comparable companies, Uncommon Wisdom, designs, produces, and consciously creates many in-house corporations and brands, including Uncommon Wisdom Publishing, Uncommon Wisdom Productions Corp., and Uncommon Wisdom Special Events, to name a few.

Currently, Kjirsten has a heart and soul-centered passion for investing in conscious corporations that help to make this world a better place for us all. She seeks to invest in precious opportunities around the world and across a wide range of asset classes that convert savings into productive capital.

PETER GIESIN

In the realm of technology, Peter stands at the forefront as the Co-Founder and Chief Technology Officer of Ignite Publishing. With a deep-rooted belief in the transformative power of digital tools, he has tirelessly dedicated himself to creating platforms that provide intuitive and powerful solutions for the publishing world.

Parallel to his technological pursuits, Peter's heart beats for literature. As a Software Evangelist, he passionately believes that every emerging author deserves a stage, and he's committed to leveraging technology to build those stages. This commitment is further evident in his own endeavors as an author, where he channels the power of words to connect, inspire, and challenge the norm.

Beyond the binaries of the digital world and the eloquence of written tales, Peter's spirit of adventure takes center stage. Whether it's hiking uncharted territories, diving into the depths of the ocean, or exploring age-old cultures, he's on a ceaseless quest to understand the breadth of human potential.

Delving further into personal aspirations, Peter is ambitiously set on a personal goal: to live to 125 years old. This isn't merely about marking time; it's a testament to his unwavering passion for exploring the far limits of living a long and vital life. Always in pursuit of knowledge that can unlock the secrets of longevity and vitality, he intertwines this ambition with his adventures, technological pursuits, and literary engagements. Through his multifaceted journey, Peter not only challenges the traditional boundaries of lifespan but also inspires others to imbue every moment with vibrancy and purpose.

PHOTO CREDITS

Belinda Schroeder - *Marena Chance*
Eric Longoria - *Doten Photography*
JB Owen - *Agus Putu Pranayoga*
Kanika Rose Raney - *Danielle Finney, D. Finney Photography*
Karen R. Rosser - *Joshua Alfonso*
Kathy Stubbs - *David Jensen Photography*
Kjirsten Sigmund - *Dirk Heydemann*
Liora Karps - *Aimee Place*
Lorena Norman - *Mary DuPrie Studio*
Loretta M. Mitchell - *Nicole Noyce of Noyce Photography*
Nicole S. Freeman - *Mike The Cameraman*
Nicole Mixdorf - *Miguel & Solana Torres, Soulmate Wedding Photography*
Randy Dick - *Subaj Rakker, Akira Media Marketing*
Peter Giesin - *Kersti Niglas*
Sharni Quinn - *Jacki Bruniquel*
Tina Hatch - *Lace Andersen*
Xila C. Hope - *Isaiah & Akeyla Smith, HIS Wingspan*
Yeliz Rugar - *Yeliz Ruzgar*

THANK YOU

Thank you for being a part of the magical journey of Ignite!

Everything we do is for you, the reader, and we thank you for taking the time to enjoy and cherish these stories; and for opening your hearts and minds to the idea of igniting your own lives. We know that when one person touches the life of another, we create a ripple effect of change. That change will uplift hearts, awaken minds, and transform ideas into empowering action steps. We commit to being the leader in empowerment publishing and making sure our message inspires others in a way that will positively impact all of Humanity.

A deep appreciation also goes to each and every author who made *Ignite Your Courage* possible. It is their powerful and inspiring stories, along with their passion and desire to help others, that will Ignite Courage within each and every one of us. It takes courage to share a vulnerable part of yourself, and each one of the people in this book exemplifies that. They stepped up to share their stories for the very first time. They courageously revealed the many layers of themselves and exposed their weaknesses as few individual leaders do. Additionally, they spoke authentically from the heart and wrote what was true for them. We could have taken their stories and made them perfect, following every editing rule, but we chose instead to leave their unique and honest voices intact. We overlooked the exactness to foster individual expression. These are their words, their sentiments, and their explanations. We let their personalities shine in their writing so you would get a true sense of who each one of them is. That's what makes Ignite so unique. Authors serving others. Stories igniting humanity.

A tremendous thank you goes to all those on the Ignite team who have been working tirelessly in the background, teaching, editing, supporting, and encouraging the authors to reach the finish line. These individuals are some of the most genuine and heart-centered people I know. Their dedication to the vision of Ignite, along with their integrity and the message they convey, is of the highest caliber possible. They each want you to find inspiration and use the many Ignite Moments in this book to rise and flourish. They all believe in you, and that's what makes them so outstanding. Their dream is for all of your dreams to come true.

Production Team: JB Owen, Peter Giesin, Katie Smetherman, Mimi Safiyah, Kristine Joy Magno, and Carolina Gold.

Editing Team: Alex Blake, Michiko Couchman, JB Owen, Mimi Safiyah, Zoe Wong, and Sarah Cross.

Project Leaders: Steph Elliott, Peter Giesin, and Kjirsten Sigmund.

A special thanks and gratitude to the entire team for their support behind the scenes and for going 'above and beyond' to make this a wonderful experience. Their dedication made sure that everything ran smoothly, and with elegance.

We welcome you to share your story and become a new author in one of our upcoming books. Your message and your Ignite Moment may be exactly what someone else needs to read to Ignite their life. Readers become authors, and we want that for you. Go to www.Make.life to apply to write your story.

WRITE YOUR STORY
IN AN IGN*i*TE BOOK

THE ROAD TO SHARING YOUR MESSAGE AND BECOMIN A BEST-SELLING AUTHOR BEGINS RIGHT HERE.

We make YOU a best-selling author in just four months

If you have a story of perseverance, determination, growth, awakening, and change... and you've felt the power of your Ignite Moment, we'd love to hear from you.

We are always looking for motivating stories that will make a difference in someone's life. fun, enjoyable, four-month writing process is like no other—and the best thing about IGNI the community of outstanding, like-minded individuals dedicated to helping others.

With over 700 amazing individuals to date writing their stories and sharing their Ignite Mor we are positively impacting the planet and raising the vibration of HUMANITY. Our stories i and empower others and we want to add your story to one of our upcoming books!

Go to our website, click How To Get Started, and share a bit of your Ignite transformatic

JOIN US TO IGNITE A BILLION LIVES WITH A BILLION WORDS.

Apply at: www.igniteyou.life/apply   Find out more at: www.igniteyou.

Inquire at: info@igniteyou.life

Printed in the USA
CPSIA information can be obtained
at www.ICGtesting.com
LVHW051731281023
R17945000002B/R179450PG762208LVX00002B/1